# PUB STROLLS IN
# SOMERSET

Anne-Marie Edwards

COUNTRYSIDE BOOKS
NEWBURY BERKSHIRE

First published 2004
© Anne-Marie Edwards 2004

COUNTRYSIDE BOOKS
3 Catherine Road
Newbury, Berkshire

To view our complete range of books,
please visit us at
www.countrysidebooks.co.uk

ISBN 1 85306 830 6

*Pour nos chers amis, Janine et Pascal*

Designed by Graham Whiteman
Photographs by Mike Edwards

Typeset by Techniset Typesetters, Newton-le-Willows
Produced through MRM Associates Ltd., Reading
Printed by Woolnough Bookbinding Ltd., Irthlingborough

# Contents

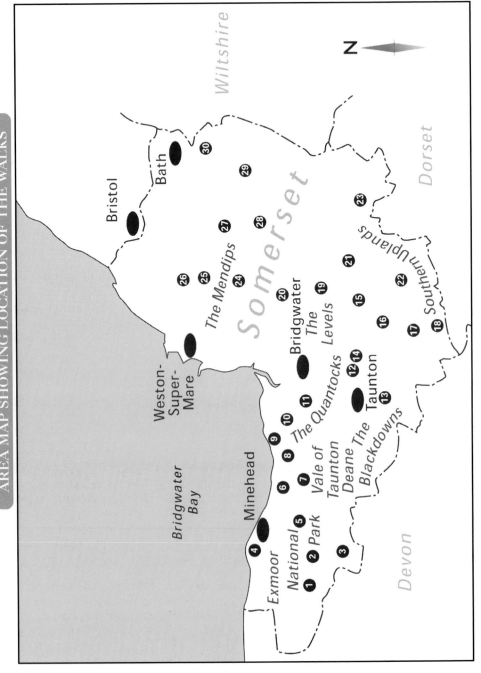

# PUBLISHER'S NOTE

We hope that you obtain considerable enjoyment from this book; great care has been taken in its preparation. However, changes of landlord and actual closures are sadly not uncommon. Likewise, although at the time of publication all routes followed public rights of way or permitted paths, diversion orders can be made and permissions withdrawn.

We cannot, of course, be held responsible for such diversion orders and any inaccuracies in the text which result from these or any other changes to the routes nor any damage which might result from walkers trespassing on private property. We are anxious though that all details covering the walks and the pubs are kept up to date and would therefore welcome information from readers which would be relevant to future editions.

The simple sketch maps that accompany the walks in the book are based on notes made by the author whilst checking out the routes on the ground. For the benefit of a proper map, however, we do recommend that you purchase the relevant Ordnance Survey sheet covering your walk. The Ordnance Survey maps are widely available, especially through booksellers and local newsagents.

Do you feel, in these days of hustle and bustle with everything always changing, a need to get away from it all, to forget about coping with traffic and paying bills, and find some quiet place that only changes with the seasons, is soothingly peaceful and always beautiful and interesting? If you do, come strolling in Somerset!

No county could be more rewarding for the walker. The dramatic coastline rises to over 1,000 feet, the highest cliffs in England. In the west, most of Exmoor, still a wilderness of rolling moorland and deep leafy combes, lies within the county's bounds. South-east of Exmoor rise the wooded Blackdown Hills, giving spectacular views over to the lush vale of Taunton Deane and the steep slopes of the Quantocks. In the east, the porous limestone of the Mendips has resulted in spectacular caves and gorges, the home of prehistoric man. The southern uplands, forming the county's border with Dorset, shelter beautiful villages built of golden stone from Ham Hill. In the heart of the county lie the Levels, one of Europe's most important wetlands, rich in rare plants.

But glorious scenery is only part of the charm of Somerset. The county is famous for its churches built with the profits from the wool trade during the 14th and 15th centuries. Splendid towers rising to battlements and fountains of crocketed pinnacles grace the countryside. Stately homes and gardens, many owned by the National Trust, await discovery. It is a county of romance, history and legend. Everywhere you will hear tales of Arthur and his fabled Camelot.

Wildlife flourishes in this quiet county. Ponies and herds of red deer roam Exmoor and the Quantocks, the soft red earth of sunken paths and lanes provides homes for badgers and foxes, buzzards wheel mewing overhead. The wetlands of the Levels are a paradise for all water-loving birds, so remember your binoculars!

Although in the past other industries apart from the wool trade, such as the mining of lead in the Mendips and iron ore in the Brendons, brought prosperity to Somerset, it was always predominantly a farming county and still is today. The most fertile area is the vale of Taunton Deane dotted with scattered villages where cows stand knee deep in the grass and sheep graze beneath the apple trees. Here you can sample cider made in the traditional fashion and enjoy the finest of cream teas.

A visit to a good pub combined with a stroll in lovely countryside makes a day even more rewarding. The strolls in this book – with one exception – start at, or close to, an excellent pub chosen for its ales, home-cooking and welcoming atmosphere. The exception is Periwinkle Cottage at Selworthy where there are no pubs. Once you have walked in this glorious part of Exmoor and enjoyed a visit to the Cottage, famous for its cakes and pastries, I am sure you will allow me this one omission! I include details of what food and drink are available at each establishment, together with opening times and telephone numbers. When a pub car park is mentioned, publicans are happy to allow patrons to leave cars while they walk but they do ask us to seek their permission first. There is also a note on places of interest nearby so that you can extend your day out if you wish.

*Anne-Marie Edwards*

# Withypool
## In the heart of Exmoor
### *The Royal Oak Inn*

**MAP:** OS OUTDOOR LEISURE 9 EXMOOR (GR 845355)

**WALK 1**

**DISTANCE:** 4½ MILES

**DIRECTIONS TO START:** WITHYPOOL LIES A MILE WEST OF THE B3223 LYNTON TO DULVERTON ROAD. AFTER TURNING OFF THE B3223 DRIVE THROUGH THE VILLAGE PAST THE ROYAL OAK INN. THE ROAD CURVES LEFT TO CROSS A BRIDGE OVER THE RIVER BARLE AND THE CAR PARK IS ON YOUR RIGHT. **PARKING:** IN THE PUBLIC CAR PARK.

This walk is a little longer than our other pub strolls but it is so beautiful that I could not resist including it. We start from Withypool, a genuine old world village cradled in a moorland hollow. In medieval days it was an important place, the 'capital' of the Royal Forest of Exmoor. The present church with its squat tower was rebuilt in the late 19th century but inside the church has retained its simply carved Norman font. From the village we follow part of the Two Moors Way, heading south beside the River Barle. Our return route leaves the valley to take a high moorland track to Comer's Cross on the B3223 where we turn left to walk downhill to the village.

## The Royal Oak Inn

For over three hundred years this friendly hostelry has provided refreshment for the villagers and welcomed travellers. The two comfortably furnished bars with their low beamed ceilings and crackling wintertime log fires are decorated with sporting prints and paintings and shining copper and brass ornaments. There is a large separate dining room. In 1866 R.D. Blackmore wrote part of his famous novel *Lorna Doone* at the inn. Soon after D-day General Eisenhower stayed here. A former owner, Maxwell Knight, was the spy-master upon whom the character of 'M', James Bond's boss, was based.

Everything on the menu is home-made and ranges from snacks such as sandwiches and soup with crusty bread to imaginative dishes which, when we called, included loin of wild boar with caramelised apple sauce, venison sausages and chicken and bean cassoulet with herbs and red wine. From the sweet menu we were tempted by cheesecake with chocolate and Grand Marnier.

Real ales include Exmoor and Stag and there is a well-chosen wine list. Accommodation is available and there are two self-catering cottages.

Opening times are from 11 am (12 noon on Sundays) to 2.30 pm and from 6 pm to 11 pm. Meals are served from 12 noon to 2 pm and from 6.30 pm to 9.30 pm. Telephone: 01643 831506/7.

## The Walk

① Turn left from the car park entrance, cross the River Barle and walk through the

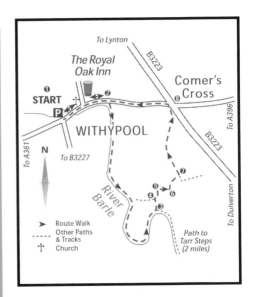

village, passing the Royal Oak on your left. Follow the road uphill for about 200 yards to a stile on your right.

② Cross the stile and follow the narrow path along the hillside as it bears left with a beautiful view over the Barle valley. Cross the next stile and continue along the hillside. After crossing two more stiles the path follows the hillside above the river for a short distance then descends to run through the meadows beside the river. Pass the stepping stones on your right, go through a gate and continue along the riverside. The path rises as you go through a gate to walk through woods then another gate opens to meadowland. Keep ahead over the grass, still following the path, which descends to run beside the river once more and curves left through woodland.

Look carefully through the trees a little to your left for a small fingerpost which indicates the point where we leave the river.

*Stepping stones over the Barle near Withypool*

③ Turn left, following the bridleway for Winsford Hill, and walk uphill with a stream on your right. Go through a gate and continue up the valley to a cross-track.

④ Turn right, signed 'Winsford Hill', to cross the stream then bear left as the sign directs. The stream is on your left. The path climbs the hillside.

⑤ When you are almost at the top turn right to go through a small wooden gate. Keep straight on with a hedge on your right. Go through the next gate to meet an asphalt track.

⑥ Turn left and follow the track as it leads gently uphill rewarding you with wide moorland views.

### PLACES OF INTEREST NEARBY

**Tarr Steps** is an ancient clapper bridge over the River Barle about 4 miles south of Withypool. Turn west for the bridge off the B3223. Nearby there is a car park and Tarr Farm is now an inn.

⑦ Cross a cattle grid and turn left to follow a track over the open moor. As you approach the main road, the B3223, bear left over a cattle grid to continue over the grass beside the road. Look left for a splendid view of Withypool in the valley.

⑧ At the crossroads – Comer's Cross – turn left to walk down to the village and return to your car.

# Winsford
## A walk in the Exe valley
# *The Royal Oak Inn*

**MAP:** OS OUTDOOR LEISURE 9 EXMOOR (GR 906349)

**WALK 2**

**DISTANCE:** 2½ MILES

**DIRECTIONS TO START:** THE BEST APPROACH IS VIA THE A396, THE MINEHEAD TO TIVERTON ROAD. TURN OFF FOR WINSFORD ABOUT 4 MILES SOUTH OF WHEDDON CROSS AND DRIVE INTO THE VILLAGE.
**PARKING:** IN THE PUBLIC CAR PARK OPPOSITE THE SERVICE STATION.

Winsford, set deep in the lovely valley of the Exe, is many people's favourite Somerset village. In *Afoot in England* the naturalist W.H. Hudson wrote that Winsford is 'second to no English village in beauty; with its hoary church tower, its great trees, its old stone thatched cottages draped in ivy and vine, its soothing sound of running waters'. Here the Winn Brook flows into the Exe and to explore the village you must cross no fewer than eight bridges! This walk around West Howe Hill follows woodland paths through the Exe valley past the attractive hamlet of West Howetown to Coppleham, another tiny hamlet, then climbs the hill to return to Winsford. The climb is short but steep and you may prefer to retrace your steps along the valley.

## The Royal Oak Inn

A village as attractive as Winsford deserves an equally attractive inn, and the Royal Oak, which dates from the 12th century, fits the picture perfectly with its white walls beneath a darkly-thatched roof, inglenook fireplaces and old oak beams. And you can be assured of a warm welcome, whether you settle for one of the two comfortably furnished bars or the spacious restaurant.

A wide range of bar snacks is on offer and a superb menu which, when we called, included lamb shank braised in red wine, and supreme of chicken wrapped in Parma ham. Home-made puddings included rhubarb and apple crumble and chocolate truffle. Real ales are Brakspear Bitter and Butcombe Bitter and a guest ale from Cotleigh or Exmoor. Overnight accommodation is available.

Opening times are from 11 am to 2.30 pm (Sundays from 12 noon to 3 pm) and from 7 pm to 11 pm. Meals are served from 12 noon to 2 pm and from 7 pm to 9 pm. Telephone: 01643 851455.

## The Walk

① Turn right from the car park entrance, passing the service station and phone box on your left. We intend taking the next lane on the left but first look over the road opposite the post office. Marked with a plaque is the cottage where Ernest Bevin, Minister of Labour during the Second World War, was born in 1881.

② With the post office on your right, turn down the lane to cross the bridge over the Exe. If you peer into the bushes below

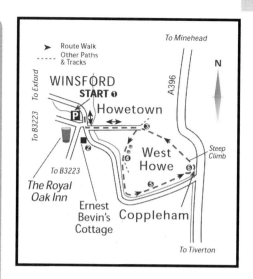

you on the left you may be able to see where the Winn joins the Exe. Follow the lane past the playing field. In the south-east corner stands the Bevin Oak, planted in 1981 by the respected trade union leader Jack Jones CH to commemorate the centenary of Bevin's birth.

Continue along the lane through West Howetown and follow the stony track ahead uphill to a signpost.

③ Turn right, following the sign 'Bridleway to Coppleham' through a gate. Ignore the sign pointing left indicating a footpath and turn sharp right down the hill with a hedge on your right to walk along the foot of the field. Go through an iron gate and follow the track ahead through a small wooden gate. The path leads downhill, bearing left through oak and beech woods, with the Exe winding through the valley on your right.

④ Go through another small wooden gate and when the path divides bear right downhill to go through a gate. Keep ahead

*Winsford*

over a narrow field, passing a private bridge on your right, and continue with the river on your right and the wooded hillside on your left for about 400 yards through two gates.

⑤ Look carefully for a small wooden gate on your left. Go through it and turn right to resume your original heading with a fence and hedge on your right. Go through an iron gate and keep ahead along the foot of a field with the hedge still on your right. When you come to the corner of the hedge follow the path uphill to go through a gate. Follow the terraced path ahead as it leads down towards the river. Go through gates each side of a track and continue along the terraced path to a junction. Turn right here downhill, following the bridleway sign. Go through a gate and continue with a fence on your right to go through the next gate and over a drive in Coppleham. Cross the grass, go through another gate and continue with a fence still on your right to a track.

⑥ Turn left uphill, following the footpath sign for Winsford. Go through a gate and continue uphill and over a stile. Climb the steep hillside ahead with a hedge on your left. Cross the stile at the top and keep ahead, with the hedge still on your left, to go through a gate. Bear a little left with the hedge still on your left and the hillside descending steeply on your right. Go through the middle gate of the three ahead (signed footpath) and continue, with a hedge now on your right. The next gate opens to a clear track. Follow this, still with a hedge on your right. Ignore a small wooden gate on your right and continue beside the hedge to walk down the hill to rejoin our earlier path at the gate near point 3. Go through the gate and retrace your steps back to Winsford.

## PLACES OF INTEREST NEARBY
The bridge at **Tarr Steps** (see Walk 1) is to the south-west of Winsford, across the B3223.

# Dulverton
## The southern gateway to Exmoor
# *The Bridge Inn*

**MAP:** OS OUTDOOR LEISURE 9 EXMOOR
(GR 913278)

**WALK 3**

**DISTANCE:** $3\frac{1}{2}$ MILES

**DIRECTIONS TO START:** THE BEST APPROACH IS VIA THE M5. LEAVE AT JUNCTION 27 ALONG THE A361, SIGNED TO TIVERTON. AFTER ABOUT 6 MILES TURN RIGHT AT A ROUNDABOUT ONTO THE A396, SIGNED TO DULVERTON. TURN LEFT ALONG THE B3222, WHICH BEARS RIGHT TO CROSS THE BRIDGE OVER THE RIVER BARLE INTO DULVERTON. **PARKING:** IMMEDIATELY AFTER CROSSING THE BRIDGE TURN LEFT TO DRIVE PAST THE FIRE STATION TO A LARGE CAR PARK ON YOUR RIGHT.

Dulverton owes its name to the Saxons who called their new home 'the settlement by the hidden ford'. Today this small town, built up a slope east of the River Barle and surrounded on three sides by steep wooded hills, still retains a charming village atmosphere. The busy High Street, lined by attractive shops and cottages, is overlooked by the town hall, which was built in the 18th century and has an unusual external staircase. From the town we follow woodland paths with splendid views over the Barle valley and the Exmoor hills to a packhorse bridge over a tributary of the river at the junction of several narrow lanes. We cross the Barle, then follow the valley path through the old oaks and beeches of Burridge Wood to return to Dulverton.

## The Bridge Inn

This friendly inn beside the Barle is the perfect introduction to this lovely part of Somerset. It has been the landlord's home for many years and you are welcomed as one of the family. The bar area is comfortably furnished and there is a separate restaurant. In fine weather you can sit outside on the terrace with a delightful view over the medieval bridge to Burridge Wood.

Real ales are Tetley Cask, Marston's Pedigree and Greene King's Abbot Ale. Appetising home-cooked food includes Cumberland sausage whirl, steak and kidney pie, ham cut off the bone, and steaks with a choice of sauces. A wide range of ploughman's and sandwiches is available and among the satisfying sweets when we called were blackcurrant cheesecake and treacle sponge pudding.

Opening times are from 11 am to 2.30 pm and from 6 pm to 11 pm. Meals are served from 12 noon to 2 pm and from 6 pm to 9 pm. Telephone: 01398 323694.

## The Walk

① Turn left from the car park entrance. The large building beside the river on your right is the former workhouse, now the headquarters of the Exmoor National Park Authority. The statue of Lorna Doone is a reminder that R.D. Blackmore set many scenes in his famous novel in Dulverton. When you come to the bridge, turn left past the Bridge Inn to walk up the High Street. At the Y-junction take the left hand road (Fore Street), signed for Exford and

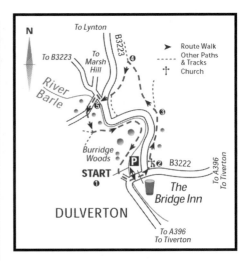

Lynton, past the Exmoor National Park Visitor Centre. Walk up to the church to the south gateway. Among much of interest, the church houses a marvellous collection of tapestry kneelers.

② Continue past the gateway on your left and bear a little left across some cobbles to follow a lane which climbs between walls to a T-junction. Turn left up the hill and after about 50 yards by the Old School House turn right up a track running between high hedges typical of Exmoor. They are built of stones placed vertically, then mounded with earth and planted with trees. We came this way in spring and the banks were thickly carpeted with primroses, violets and early bluebells. The track winds uphill through oak and beech woods past a footpath on the left.

③ Opposite a white gate on the right our track bears left to continue uphill through more open country with wonderful views. Keep ahead, following the footpath sign for Broford, until just past a bench on the right you come to a signpost.

*The packhorse bridge over a tributary of the Barle*

④ Turn left, following the sign for Marsh Bridge steeply downhill. When the track divides keep straight on (right hand track), still downhill. Cross straight over the road, the B3223, and keep ahead to cross a lane to the packhorse bridge over a small stream flowing into the Barle. This is the ideal place for a picnic!

⑤ Bear left to cross the rather larger bridge over the Barle up the lane, following the sign 'Footpath to Dulverton'. After about 250 yards, just before the lane curves right, bear left along the footpath signed for Dulverton. Pass some farm buildings, go through a gate and follow the path across the valley past a farm to a post indicating two footpaths, one ahead and one to the right. Do not take either but turn left between wooden rails to continue in the direction of Dulverton along a wide path, with the trees of Burridge Wood rising steeply on your right and the river running through the meadows on your left. The path rises and falls, still following the river, eventually to meet a lane. Continue downhill to the bridge in Dulverton and turn left to cross the bridge and return to your car.

### PLACES OF INTEREST NEARBY

The **Guildhall Heritage and Arts Centre** near the car park in Dulverton is packed with interest including displays detailing Dulverton's history, Granny Baker's Cottage and exhibitions of local arts and crafts. Admission is free and the Centre is open from the end of March to the beginning of November. For further information telephone the Exmoor National Park Visitor Centre: 01398 323841.

# Selworthy
## In the coastal hills
# *Periwinkle Cottage and Tea Rooms*

**MAP:** OS OUTDOOR LEISURE 9 EXMOOR (GR 920468)

**WALK 4**

**DISTANCE:** 2½ MILES

**DIRECTIONS TO START:** SELWORTHY LIES IN THE HILLS OVERLOOKING THE EXMOOR COAST, ABOUT 4½ MILES WEST OF MINEHEAD. TURN FOR THE VILLAGE OFF THE A39. **PARKING:** IN THE CAR PARK OPPOSITE THE CHURCH. DRIVE UPHILL THROUGH THE VILLAGE. THE ROAD CURVES RIGHT TO THE CHURCH ON THE LEFT AND THE CAR PARK ON THE RIGHT. IF THIS IS FULL CONTINUE STRAIGHT ON FOR ABOUT 75 YARDS TO THE OVERFLOW CAR PARK.

No visit to Exmoor is complete without a walk around Selworthy! It must be everyone's idea of a perfect English village with its wealth of thatched cottages, lime-washed and tinted cream, surrounded by flowers and immaculately mown lawns. The church stands on the hillside above the village with a splendid view over the Vale of Porlock to Dunkery Beacon crowning Exmoor's highest hill. Originally the village was part of the 12,000 acre Holnicote estate, which was owned for two hundred years by the Acland family, but in 1944 Sir Richard Acland gave the estate to the National Trust. Our walk leads uphill through woodland to enjoy a stunning view before descending Holnicote Combe and returning to Selworthy along an old packhorse track.

## Periwinkle Cottage and Tea Rooms

Selworthy is so lovely I had to include it in the book, but as Sir Thomas Dyke Acland would have no pubs on his estate – he provided his workers with reading rooms instead – I suggest you call at Periwinkle Cottage. Dating from the 16th century and heavily thatched, this teashop is one of several picturesque cottages grouped around Selworthy Green which were renovated by Sir Thomas in 1828 to provide comfortable homes for retired servants. Here you can enjoy morning coffee, a light lunch and a delicious assortment of home-made cakes and pastries. Cakes are the Cottage speciality and new ones are being constantly added to their already comprehensive list. In fine weather all this can be enjoyed in the pretty garden with views over Exmoor.

The Cottage is open from mid March to the end of October from 10.30 am till 5 pm. It is closed on Mondays, except bank holidays (closed on the Tuesdays following bank holidays). Telephone: 01643 862769. In winter, one must travel to Porlock for refreshment, an easy drive of about $2^{1}/_{2}$ miles.

### The Walk

① Turn left from the car park along the road. The church is on your right and inside there is much to admire, especially the Perpendicular south aisle with its delicately carved window tracery, slender wreathed pillars and fine wagon roof. Before the road swings left go through a small wooden gate to Selworthy Green.

An excellent National Trust shop and Information Centre is on your left. Follow the path round the gardens surrounding the cottages. Periwinkle Cottage is over the lawns on your left.

Retrace your steps through the gate.

② Turn immediately left up a stony track signed for Selworthy Beacon and Bury Castle. Continue through a gate to enter Selworthy Woods. These beautiful broad-leaved woodlands were planted by Sir Thomas, who chose a different area for each of his nine children. When the track divides take the upper right hand track and continue uphill.

③ After about $^{1}/_{4}$ mile the track divides again. Take the left hand track, following the sign for Selworthy Beacon, to cross a stream then continue uphill through the woods. As you near the top of the hill the track becomes a grassy path and bears left through pine trees to open moorland. Keep ahead past a narrow path on the left for Bury Castle. Now look left through the pine trees and you will see a small, stone-built, four-sided hut with sheltered

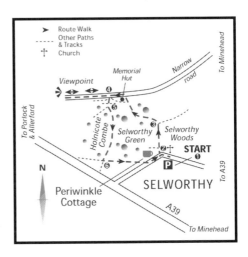

*The magnificent view from the parking area, Selworthy Beacon*

alcoves. This 'wind and weather' hut commemorates Sir Thomas, who brought his children and grandchildren here on Sunday walks. It was built in 1878 by his youngest surviving son and inscribed with verses by Keble and other poets.

After visiting the hut return to the path and turn left to continue along a road. Pass a bridleway to Allerford (our return route later in the walk) and follow the road to a parking area, a magnificent viewpoint. Westwards a long line of wooded cliffs slopes down from the hills of Exmoor to the sea. Across the Bristol Channel the hills of Wales fringe the horizon.

Retrace your steps to the bridleway for Allerford.

④ Turn right past a barrier along the grassy path leading downhill (not the gravelled 'easy access' path which at first runs to the right of the bridleway) and continue downhill over a crosspath. About 50 yards further on you will see a path leading steeply downhill on the left (unsigned).

⑤ Turn left to follow this path, which leads through a gate and becomes a stony track descending Holnicote Combe. Several paths lead left to Selworthy but for a change of scenery continue downhill for about $^{3}/_{4}$ mile to a crosspath. At this point there is a brown National Trust sign for Selworthy Woods on your right, a gate about 30 yards ahead and another gate a few yards away on your left.

⑥ Go through the gate on your left to a signpost beside a crosstrack, the cobbled packhorse road. Bear left for Selworthy. Follow the track between high hedges then across a farmyard to meet the road in Selworthy village. Turn left up the road past the 13th century tithe barn on the right and the gate leading to Selworthy Green on the left to return to your car.

## PLACES OF INTEREST NEARBY

**Allerford Museum** (also known as the **West Somerset Rural Life Museum**), west of Selworthy via the A39, includes a fully equipped Victorian kitchen and schoolroom. There is a riverside garden and a picnic area. Open Good Friday to October, weekdays 10.30 am to 1 pm, 2 pm to 4.30 pm (afternoons only on Saturdays) and on most Sundays in the school holidays. Telephone: 01643 862529.

# Luxborough (Kingsbridge)

## Woodland ways in the Brendon Hills

# *The Royal Oak Inn*

**MAP:** OS OUTDOOR LEISURE 9 EXMOOR (GR 984377)

**WALK 5**

**DISTANCE:** 3 MILES

**DIRECTIONS TO START:** LUXBOROUGH IS A LARGE PARISH IN THE HEART OF THE BRENDON HILLS. THE PARISH INCLUDES KINGSBRIDGE WHERE WE START THIS WALK. THE BEST APPROACH FROM THE NORTH IS VIA THE A39. TURN OFF SOUTHWARDS IN WASHFORD FOR ROADWATER THEN CONTINUE, HEADING WEST, FOR ABOUT 4 MILES TO KINGSBRIDGE. DRIVE PAST THE INN TO THE LARGE PUBLIC CAR PARK ON YOUR RIGHT. APPROACHING FROM THE SOUTH TURN NORTH FOR LUXBOROUGH (KINGSBRIDGE) OFF THE B3224. AFTER ABOUT 2 MILES THE CAR PARK IS ON YOUR LEFT. **PARKING:** IN THE PUBLIC CAR PARK.

Kingsbridge is a small hamlet clustered around a bridge over the Washford River. It is set in a wide green valley. Steep wooded hillsides descend to lush pastures typical of the Brendons. Sunken lanes bordered with flowers ramble over the hills, linking the small settlements within this scattered parish. We follow a woodland path, then a lane to the oldest hamlet, Churchtown, and visit the ancient church of St Mary, high on the southern slope of Croydon Hill with glorious views over Exmoor. We climb another sunken track with far-reaching views over the Washford valley before descending through woodland to return to Kingsbridge.

## The Royal Oak Inn

This delightful pub dates back to the 14th century. It is full of character with low beams, inglenook fireplaces, flagstones in the public bar and two dining rooms. The atmosphere is friendly and welcoming and we were not surprised to hear that the ghost of a little old lady with a mob cap potters about in one of the bedrooms, obviously reluctant to leave her home.

Real ales are Cotleigh Tawny, Exmoor Gold and Palmers IPA and 200. The menu offers a wide choice of snacks and full meals. The emphasis is on fresh food, which as far as possible is sourced locally. Fish is a speciality and among other choices when we called was whole roasted John Dory stuffed with lemon and herbs. Other dishes included grilled rib-eye steak and Stilton, and roast fillet of pork in cider.

Opening times are from 12 noon to 2.30 pm and from 6 pm to 11 pm. Meals are served from 12 noon to 2 pm and from 7 pm to 9 pm. Overnight accommodation is also available. Telephone: 01984 640319.

## The Walk

① Turn left from the car park entrance then turn left again over the bridge up the lane signed for Timberscombe and Dunster. A few yards further on, opposite the pub car park, turn left, following the footpath sign along a narrow path with wooden rails on your left. Cross a stile and bear left down to the stream. Bear right and walk along the foot of the field with the stream on your left for about 100 yards.

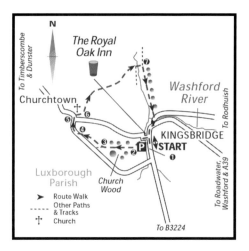

② Look for a stile on your left. Cross this and go over a footbridge to a clear path running through woods. Turn right and follow the path through the trees. This is Church Wood and it is interesting that it is planted at intervals with yews, so often associated with churchyards. Woods carpeted with wild daffodils in spring slope down to the stream on your right. Just past a house the path runs uphill and divides.

③ Take the right hand lower path and keep ahead to continue along a stony track. Pass more houses a little way down the slope on your right and walk uphill to meet a lane.

④ Bear right down the lane into the valley. Churchtown is on the opposite hillside. Follow the lane as it curves right over the stream and climbs towards Churchtown. Continue past a lane on your right.

⑤ A few yards after your lane curves left, turn right beside a stone wall on the right to the south porch of the church. This

*The Washford Valley in the Brendon Hills*

tiny church, its simple 13th century chancel lit by slender lancet windows, is well worth a visit. In the churchyard there is a fragment of a Norman or possibly Saxon cross.

With the church on your left, cross the churchyard along a grassy path and go through a gate to a lane.

⑥ Turn left to follow the lane, which soon becomes a sunken track leading uphill. At the top the path levels then descends to a gate. Go through the gate and follow the track downhill into the valley. The track curves left to cross a stream. Go through a gate and follow the track ahead, which curves right to a crosstrack.

**PLACES OF INTEREST NEARBY**
**Wimbleball Lake Water Park**, reached by turning south off the B3224, offers a wide variety of outdoor activities. For details contact the Ranger. Telephone: 01398 371372 from April to October. A gift and tea shop is open from Easter to October, 11 am to 5 pm every day. Telephone: 01398 371257.

⑦ Turn right down the track, shaded by pinewoods on the left. Eventually the track becomes asphalt and joins a lane. Turn right down the lane to the Kingsbridge road. Turn right again back to the Royal Oak and your car.

# Washford and Cleeve Abbey

## In the Vale of Flowers

## *The Washford Inn*

**MAP:** OS OUTDOOR LEISURE 9 EXMOOR (GR 044412)

**WALK 6**

**DISTANCE:** 3 MILES

**DIRECTIONS TO START:** WASHFORD IS BESIDE THE A39, NOT FAR FROM THE COAST, BETWEEN MINEHEAD AND WILLITON. DRIVE INTO THE VILLAGE AND TAKE THE TURNING FOR CLEEVE ABBEY. THE CAR PARK IS ON THE RIGHT OPPOSITE THE RUINS. **PARKING:** CLEEVE ABBEY CAR PARK.

There is something for all the family on this exciting walk. History comes alive as you explore the ruins of Cleeve Abbey (English Heritage), built by Cistercian monks and dating from the 12th century. The monks originally named their new abbey 'Vallis Florida' – 'Flowering Valley' – but later it took its name from the nearby village of Cleeve, which then became Old Cleeve. Washford was a former railhead on a Great Western Railway branch line and is now one of the beautifully maintained stations on the West Somerset Railway, which runs steam trains for twenty miles from Bishops Lydeard to Minehead. The walk also visits Old Cleeve, a charming old world village, and 16th century Washford Mill, which houses a superb collection of Somerset crafts and produce.

## The Washford Inn

The Victorians took a pride in their railways and their railway inns and the Washford Inn overlooking the station is built to the same high standard and offers the same warm welcome as it did in Victorian times. In the past the inn was popular with the drovers and dealers who thronged the cattle market opposite and it is still the centre of village life. Inside, the pub is light and spacious with large windows and plenty of room for families. There is a separate games room. You can relax in comfortable Windsor chairs while you enjoy the pub's good ales, carefully chosen wines and delicious home-cooked food. Real ales when we called were Smiles and Morland Old Speckled Hen. Included on the menu were gamekeeper's pie, steak and kidney pudding and local trout.

Opening times are from 12 noon to 11 pm and food is served from 12 noon to 2.30 pm and from 5.30 pm to 9 pm. There is a carvery on Sundays.

From the line-side garden you can watch the trains go by and children have a safe play area. Overnight accommodation is also available. Telephone: 01984 640256.

## The Walk

*If you arrive by train start from point 2 opposite the Washford Inn, turning left along the old mineral line. After your visit to Cleeve Abbey follow the directions in point 1 to return to the inn and the station.*

① From the car park follow the signed footpath with the road on your right, then

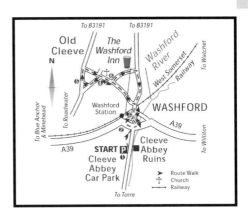

cross the road and the bridge over the little Washford River to enter the abbey precinct and go through the magnificent gatehouse. Only the footings of the walls and pillars of the cruciform priory church remain but many of the abbey's domestic buildings have survived, including the monk's refectory with its magnificent timbered roof and the 13th century dorter range comprising the sacristy, library, chapter house, parlour and warming room with the dormitory above.

Leave the abbey, cross the road and follow the path uphill, signed for Washford Mill. The path leads through woods above the mill leat and descends to the mill entrance by the road. After your visit turn left to walk up to the A39. Cross the road, turn right for a few yards then turn left down a quiet road opposite the bus stop. Turn left along Castle Mead to rejoin the A39 and turn right to face the Washford Inn.

② Just in front of the inn sign turn right along a narrow footpath signed as the old mineral line. This is part of the trackbed of the earlier West Somerset Mineral Railway, which carried ore mined in the Brendon Hills to be exported from

*A steam train arrives at Washford station, a stop on the West Somerset Railway*

Watchet to feed the iron smelters of South Wales. Continue for only about 100 yards.

③ Turn left and follow the narrow path as it curves right to bring you to a road. Bear left under the railway, climb the Monks' Steps to the left of the road, signed for Old Cleeve, and follow part of the cobbled monks' path leading to a lane. Continue up the lane, which descends to Old Cleeve church on the right. Follow the footpath on the right through the churchyard to visit the church, which is full of interest, including tiles made by the monks of Cleeve Abbey and a 15th century effigy of an unknown layman, his feet resting on a carved figure of a cat, which in turn is resting its paw on a mouse. From the churchyard there is a beautiful view over the thatched roofs of Old Cleeve to the sea.

Turn right from the church porch to go through the gate by the school.

④ Turn left past the Old Post Office and walk down to a Y-junction. Turn right downhill to a T-junction.

---

### PLACES OF INTEREST NEARBY

**Cleeve Abbey** is open all year round, from 10 am, closing at 6 pm from the end of March to the end of September, 5 pm in October, 4 pm the rest of the year. Telephone: 01984 640377.

For timetable details of the **West Somerset Railway** telephone: 01643 707650; other enquiries: 01643 704996.

For details of **Washford Mill** telephone: 01984 640412.

---

⑤ Turn right, continue past Church Farm and turn right again, signed 'Old Cleeve', uphill to rejoin your earlier route at point 4. Retrace your steps through the churchyard and up the lane to a turning for Watchet on the left.

⑥ Turn left along the lane, which runs high with more sea views, to a T-junction. Turn right for Washford to join a lane by the Monks' Steps. Retrace your route under the railway bridge, pass the footpath to the station and keep ahead, retracing your steps to the A39 and Cleeve Abbey car park.

# Monksilver
## Stately homes in the Brendon Hills
### *The Notley Arms*

**MAP:** OS OUTDOOR LEISURE 9 EXMOOR (GR 074375)

**WALK 7**

**DISTANCE:** $3\frac{1}{2}$ MILES

**DIRECTIONS TO START:** MONKSILVER IS A SMALL VILLAGE CLOSE TO THE EASTERN BOUNDARY OF THE EXMOOR NATIONAL PARK BESIDE THE B3188 WIVELISCOMBE TO WASHFORD ROAD. IT IS ALSO SIGNED OFF THE A358 TAUNTON TO WILLITON ROAD. THE NOTLEY ARMS FACES THE ROAD. **PARKING:** THE PUB CAR PARK.

Monksilver is as lovely as its name. You will discover this tiny village, just a row of pink and white cottages with colourful gardens spilling over into the road, hidden away in a valley on the eastern fringe of the Brendon Hills. In the church on the hillside Sir Walter Raleigh married his second wife, Elizabeth Sydenham, on 18th June 1583.

From the village we follow a country lane winding gently uphill to give wide views eastwards over the Quantock Hills. Then we head west along a remote valley to the site of the lost village of Nettlecombe, now the setting for Nettlecombe Court, a late-Elizabethan mansion, once the home of the Raleigh family. A streamside path leads us back to Monksilver.

## The Notley Arms

This attractive pub is deservedly popular. No bookings are taken so arrive promptly! The atmosphere is traditional with a beamed L-shaped bar, country-style settles and wooden tables and chairs. The white, half-timbered walls are decorated with original paintings. The family room has colouring books and toys for the children. Outside there is a large garden with more playthings.

An extensive menu provides meals to suit every taste. All the food is home-made with fresh locally prod-uced ingredients wherever possible. On our visit the daily blackboard included smoked mackerel, lasagne and tagliatelle with ham, mushrooms and cream. Among the wide range of 'specials' were bacon, leek and cider pudding (variations with pork or chicken), Italian-style roast pork with juniper and rosemary and red mullet fillets with orange and capers. Real ales are Exmoor Ale, Smiles Best and Wadworth 6X. Farm cider and country wines are also available.

Opening times on Monday to Satur-day are from 11.30 am to 2.30 pm and from 6.30 pm to 11 pm; 12 noon to 2.30 and 7 pm to 11 pm (10.30 in winter) on Sundays. Food is served from 12 noon to 2 pm and from 7 pm to 9.30 pm. Telephone: 01984 656217.

## The Walk

① Turn right from the front door of the pub and after about 150 yards turn right up the next lane. This curves right uphill then left past the old school house to run along the hillside between banks of wild flowers in season. The lane dips then rises past Birchanger Farm to meet Nettlecombe Park Road, another peaceful lane.

② Turn right to follow the lane as it leads downhill.

③ Just before you reach the foot of the lane turn left along the lane signed for Nettlecombe Court and church.

④ Pass a bridleway sign on your right (we follow this later) and continue along this beautiful valley, which is threaded by a small stream and dotted with magnificent oak trees. Pass a lake on your right and the gateposts of Nettlecombe Court to see this fine manor built of local rose-coloured sandstone. The house passed by marriage to the Cornish Trevelyans, whose descendant John Wolseley is the present owner. Since 1967 it has been leased to the Field Studies Council.

The church close by has many treasures including an exquisitely carved 'Seven Sacrament' font and two 13th and 14th century effigies of members of the Raleigh family.

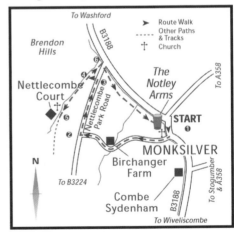

*Nettlecombe Court, once the home of Sir Walter Raleigh*

⑤ Retrace your steps for about $\frac{1}{2}$ mile to the bridleway, now on your left, at point 4. Go through the gate and follow the grassy path downhill to meet a track in the valley. Turn right to rejoin Nettlecombe Park Road.

⑥ Turn left for about 30 yards then turn right over a stile signed for Monksilver. Walk uphill towards a yellow-banded post and follow the narrow path along the hillside, keeping the steep tree-covered slope leading down to the stream on your left. The path descends, still with trees on the left, to a stile on the left. Cross the stile, go down some steps and over a dip to go over another stile. The path continues a little uphill with trees still on the left then descends to enter the trees.

⑦ Cross a stile, go over a small stream and up the bank on the other side. Continue uphill, bearing a little left. Cross the next stile and follow the path ahead through woods to go over another stile. Bear right through a gap to take a permitted path then turn left to resume your former heading towards the tower of Monksilver church with a hedge on your left. The path turns left down some steps to a track. Turn right then bear left to the main road in Monksilver. Turn right for the Notley Arms and your car.

### PLACES OF INTEREST NEARBY

**Combe Sydenham Country Park,** just south of Monksilver, is a historic Elizabethan manor house set among 500 acres of park and woodland. It offers walking and bike trails, wildlife, a working corn mill, a shop and a tea room. The Country Park is open from Easter to the end of October, Sunday to Friday, 10 am to 5 pm. For the opening times of other attractions telephone: 01984 656284.

# Bicknoller

## In the western Quantock Hills

## *The Bicknoller Inn*

**MAP:** OS EXPLORER 140 QUANTOCK HILLS AND BRIDGWATER (GR 110392)

**WALK 8**

**DISTANCE:** 2 MILES

**DIRECTIONS TO START:** BICKNOLLER IS A SMALL VILLAGE JUST OFF THE A358 TAUNTON TO WILLITON ROAD. APPROACHING FROM TAUNTON TURN RIGHT FOLLOWING THE FIRST SIGN FOR BICKNOLLER. APPROACHING FROM WILLITON TURN LEFT FOLLOWING THE SECOND SIGN FOR THE VILLAGE. SHORTLY, YOU WILL SEE THE BICKNOLLER INN ON YOUR LEFT.
**PARKING:** THE INN'S CAR PARK OPPOSITE THE INN.

The western slopes of the Quantock Hills rise more steeply than those in the east. Throughout their length the hillsides are furrowed by wooded combes sheltering villages that seem untouched by time. One of my favourites is Bicknoller. A winding lane leads past 16th and 17th century cottages, many thatched and colour-washed, to the church of St George, famous for its magnificent carved bench ends and rood screen. In the churchyard the village stocks are shaded by an enormous hollow yew. From the village we climb the hillside to enjoy wonderful views and perhaps see a mealy-nosed Exmoor pony (so called because they look as if they have dipped their noses in a bucket of wholemeal flour) or catch a glimpse of a red deer.

## The Bicknoller Inn

Simply built, with white walls beneath a roof of golden brown thatch, this old inn seems little changed since the days when coaches rattled across its cobbled courtyard. The bar area has rough stone walls, a heavily beamed ceiling and a splendid Elizabethan inglenook fireplace. There is a separate restaurant. In the inn's relaxing old world atmosphere you can sample a range of real ales including Wadworth 6X, Palmers IPA and Boddingtons Bitter. Somerset cider is also on offer and a selection of wines.

When we called, the many appetising dishes included breaded plaice stuffed with broccoli and cream cheese, salmon Bretagne, home-made curries and ham and mushroom tagliatelle.

Opening times are from 12 noon to 2 pm and from 6 pm to 11 pm. Meals are served from 12 noon to 2 pm and from 6 pm to 9 pm (9.30 pm on Fridays and Saturdays). There is a large garden behind the inn. Telephone: 01984 656234.

## The Walk

① Turn left from the front of the inn to walk up through the village to the church. A visit to this fine church is a 'must'. The bench ends showing village scenes as well as people, animals and a wealth of intricately patterned foliage are believed to be the work of a celebrated carver, Simon Warman, buried in Bicknoller in 1585. Pass the church on your right and walk up Church Lane, which curves right to a T-junction.

② Turn left, then opposite the post office turn right to walk up Hill Lane. The lane

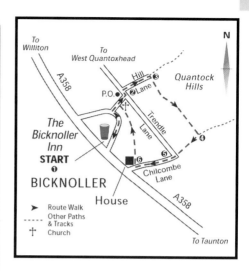

leads uphill towards rounded, bracken-covered slopes rising above oak woods. Go through a gate leading into the woods by the National Trust sign.

③ Turn immediately right up a steep slope signed for Quantock Moor (this is rather a scramble but you soon come to a good path). The route now leads along the hillside, climbing to give wide views west over Bicknoller in the valley to the Brendon Hills and north over Bridgwater Bay to the coast of Wales. The path descends to continue beside one of the high hedgebanks planted with beeches,

## PLACES OF INTEREST NEARBY

**The West Somerset Railway** runs steam trains and vintage diesels for 20 miles beside the western slopes of the Quantock Hills and along the coast from Bishops Lydeard to Minehead, stopping at Crowcombe, Stogumber, Williton, Watchet, Washford and Blue Anchor. There is a 24 hour talking timetable: 01643 707650; other enquiries: 01643 704996.

*St George slays the dragon – one of the fine carved bench ends in Bicknoller church*

asphalt lane and turn right, indicated by the Quantock Greenway sign, to follow the lane downhill over grassland and then through a wood to a Y-junction.

⑤ Keep ahead along the left hand lane – Chilcombe Lane – for about $1/4$ mile.

⑥ Just before the entrance to a house look very carefully in the hedge on your right for a post inscribed 'public footpath' (this is about 30 yards before you come to the main road). Turn right through an iron gate and keep ahead, passing close to the back of the house on your left. Cross a stile and continue over the next field to go through a gap in the hedge. Head towards the tower of Bicknoller church over another field to go over a stile by a gate. Still using the tower as your guide cross the field and go over a final stile to a lane by the church. Turn left to return to the Bicknoller Inn and your car.

which are frequently used as windbreaks on the Quantocks and Exmoor.

④ Go through a small wooden gate to an

# Kilve and East Quantoxhead

### Where the Quantock Hills meet the sea

## *The Hood Arms*

**MAP:** OS EXPLORER 140 QUANTOCK HILLS AND BRIDGWATER (GR 149429)

**WALK 9**

**DISTANCE:** 3 MILES

**DIRECTIONS TO START:** KILVE IS A SMALL VILLAGE BESIDE THE A39 MIDWAY BETWEEN MINEHEAD AND BRIDGWATER. **PARKING:** IN THE CAR PARK IN KILVE, SIGNED OFF THE MAIN ROAD.

When William Wordsworth and his sister Dorothy rented Alfoxton, a Georgian house high on the northernmost bluff of the Quantock Hills not far from the sea, Dorothy described her new surroundings with delight. 'There is everything here,' she wrote in her journal, 'sea, woods as wild as fancy ever painted ... villages so romantic.' Today very little has changed. We follow their walk to the sea. On the way we visit East Quantoxhead, surely one of Dorothy's romantic villages with its church, manor and thatched cottages clustered around a large pond. Our path takes the coast path above Kilve beach with the sheer cliffs and headlands of Bridgwater Bay rising to east and west. At the foot of the cliffs waves break against great strands of flat shale-bearing rock. We return to Kilve along a quiet lane past a ruined medieval chantry.

## The Hood Arms

This is one of Somerset's welcoming black and white coaching inns, with a cobbled courtyard and a spacious walled garden. The comfortable bars have a distinct character created by heavily beamed ceilings, large fireplaces and sturdy wooden furniture. There is a beamed function room, a cosy lounge with plush seating and a separate restaurant with a raised area overlooking the garden.

The Hood is well known for the quality of its food. Among the dishes when we called were poached salmon, pork chops in a cider sauce, venison casserole and breast of duck. Real ales are Cotleigh Tawny, Exmoor Ale and a choice of guest beers. Local farmhouse cider and a variety of wines are also available.

Opening times are from 10.30 am to 3 pm and from 6 pm to 11 pm. Food is served from 12 noon to 2.30 pm (2 pm on Sundays) and from 6 pm to 9 pm. Parties please book beforehand.

The inn offers accommodation in five double bedrooms and two self-catering mews cottages. Telephone: 01278 741210.

## The Walk

① Walk towards the entrance to the car park but do not go as far as the main road. Turn left just before you come to it along a grassy fence footpath which curves right then left to bring you to the main road. Continue beside the road (there is a narrow verge) for about 100 yards. Just before the road swings left cross the road to a footpath sign.

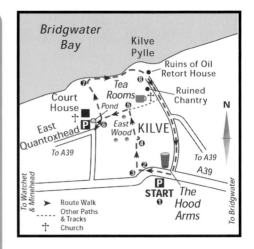

② Go over a stile and keep straight on over a field to cross another stile.

③ Turn right and continue ahead with a hedge on your right. As the path descends there are wonderful views over the fields to the sea.

④ When you reach East Wood do not enter the wood but turn right just before it through a gate. Continue for a few yards with a hedge on your left, then turn left through a gap in the hedge. Bear left to the edge of the wood, then turn right to resume your former heading northwards towards the sea. Pass a gate into the wood and continue downhill, keeping the wood on your left.

⑤ At the end of the wood turn left through a gate and follow the path to a gate opening to a track beside the gardens of Court House at East Quantoxhead.

⑥ Walk up the track with the gardens on your right to the pond in East Quantoxhead. Across the car park on your right a path leads up to the 14th

*The path to the sea from Kilve*

century church, which retains its medieval rood screen. Fortress-like Court House close by is the home of Sir Walter Fownes Luttrell, a descendant of Ralph Pagnell, who was granted the manor after the Norman Conquest.

Retrace your steps past the pond to the gate at point 6 and turn left, following the sign for the beach. Continue along the wide green way and fenced path through a gate past steps leading down to the beach.

⑦ Bear right along the coast path, much loved by the Wordsworths. William wrote of 'Kilve's delightful shore' in his poem *Anecdote for Fathers*. After a little over $1/2$ mile descend some steps to the grassy levels of Kilve Pylle. Follow the path beside a fence to cross a bridge to a tall brick building on the left. This is the remains of an oil retort house. In the mid 1920s attempts were made to extract oil from the shale but the process proved too costly and was soon abandoned.

⑧ Follow the path as it bears right and becomes an asphalt lane. On the right you pass the gaunt ruins of a chantry founded in 1329 by Sir Simon de Furneaux. It is rumoured that the chantry was destroyed by a fire fuelled by kegs of smuggled brandy! The simple grey stone church close by dates from the 13th century and has a magnificently timbered roof.

The Chantry Tea Gardens are nearby and also offer bed and breakfast. For details telephone: 01278 741457

Follow the lane to the main road, the A39, and turn right for the Hood Arms and the car park.

---

## PLACES OF INTEREST NEARBY

**Watchet**, reached via the A39 to the west, is an appealing small town and port. The **Watchet Market House Museum** houses local history and archaelogical collections. It is open at Easter and from mid May to September daily, 10.30 am to 12.30 pm, 2.30 pm to 4.30 pm. Also 7 pm to 9 pm in July and August. Telephone: 01643 707132.

# Nether Stowey

### A poets' landscape

## *The Rose & Crown*

**MAP:** OS EXPLORER 140 QUANTOCK HILLS AND BRIDGWATER (GR 190397)

**WALK 10**

**DISTANCE:** 3 MILES

**DIRECTIONS TO START:** NETHER STOWEY IS ABOUT 9 MILES NORTH-WEST OF BRIDGWATER. APPROACHING FROM BRIDGWATER ALONG THE A39 TURN FOR THE VILLAGE AND DRIVE DOWN ST MARY STREET, TO THE CLOCK TOWER AT THE JUNCTION WITH CASTLE STREET. TURN LEFT ALONG CASTLE STREET TO THE CAR PARK SIGNED ON YOUR RIGHT. **PARKING:** IN THE PUBLIC CAR PARK.

Nether Stowey is a picturesque village sheltered by the gently rising eastern slopes of the Quantock Hills. Castle Street, in the centre of the village, is particularly attractive and is lined with rows of colour-washed houses, many medieval in origin. A small stream flows down one side of the wide street, christened by Samuel Taylor Coleridge the 'dear gutter of Stowey'. In December 1796 the poet came to live in the village with his wife Sara and baby Hartley close to his benefactor, a wealthy local tanner, Thomas Poole. William and Dorothy Wordsworth moved to live nearby at Alfoxton and together they roamed the Quantock Hills composing poetry to be published later as *The Lyrical Ballads*. This is a walk in their footsteps.

## The Rose & Crown

You will enjoy the special charm and character of this friendly coaching inn. The walls are decorated with a wealth of interesting items including many colourful original paintings. Some are the work of a local artist whose studio upstairs is open for visitors. Such a delightful inn deserves an equally appealing ghost and the Rose & Crown is the home of a 'greenman'. You will see carvings of greenmen and their friends on bench ends in churches. They are believed to ensure an abundant harvest. At the Rose & Crown the greenman's efforts are obviously successful as the varied menu includes a selection of fresh vegetables straight from the garden. Among the dishes when we called were pheasant casserole, smoked haddock with chives and shallot butter, beef fillet with Stilton and port, and leek and cheese pancakes.

Real ales are changed regularly but you can rely on Otter, Moor and Cotleigh. Lane's farm cider makes a pleasant alternative. Opening times are from 12 noon to 11 pm on Monday to Saturday. On Sundays the hours are from 12 noon to 5 pm and from 7 pm to 10.30 pm. Food is served Wednesdays to Sundays, from 12 noon to 2.30 pm and from 7.30 pm to 9 pm (last orders 8.45 pm). Overnight accommodation is also available. Telephone: 01278 732265 (groups please book beforehand).

## The Walk

① Turn right from the car park up Castle Street. The road runs uphill to a fork at the foot of the Mount, the site of an 11th century motte and bailey castle.

② Take the left hand road as it begins to curve round the Mount and turn right, following a footpath sign. Cross a stile and climb the earthworks of the castle to enjoy a magnificent view over Bridgwater Bay to the coast of Wales. Retrace your steps to the road and turn right to resume your former heading. Follow the road as it curves left for about 200 yards to Hockpitt Lane on your left.

③ Turn left along Hockpitt Lane. Pass Hockpitt Farm and keep straight on over a stile, following a hedged footpath. Cross two V-shaped stiles and keep ahead with a hedge on the right. Cross double stiles

*Nether Stowey. The clock tower commemorates Queen Victoria's Silver Jubilee*

and continue ahead towards the tower of Over Stowey church. Pass Cross Farm on your left and go over a stile to a lane.

④ Cross the lane and take the lane almost ahead of you leading to Over Stowey, leaving a tree-crowned mound on your right. The lane curves left round the church. Our way is along the footpath to the right off the corner past The Coach House. But before continuing the walk call in to the little church of Saints Peter and Paul. It has a fine set of carved bench ends typical of the Quantocks, and a

monument commemorating two Rich brothers, depicting farming symbols.

⑤ Turn right along the footpath indicated above, past The Coach House, and follow it as it curves right. Cross a stile on the left and continue over a field with a hedge on your right. Follow the line of the hedge as it curves right, cross double stiles then bear left to resume your former heading with the hedge now on your left. Cross the next stile and continue up the field. Cross stiles to go through a small coppice and keep ahead to cross another stile. Continue up the field then bear right to go through a gate to a lane.

⑥ Turn right along the lane for about ¼ mile to a bridleway sign on your right.

⑦ Bear right along this narrow, hedged path which sinks between banks of wild flowers. Badgers have tunnelled deep into the soft red earth.

⑧ When you meet a lane turn left then take the first lane on the right, which runs downhill with a view of the Mount ahead.

⑨ Take the next lane on the right (marked with weight restriction signs) and follow it as it curves left to pass Hockpitt Lane and join your outbound route. Retrace your steps down Castle Street to your car. To visit the Rose & Crown follow Castle Street to the junction with Lime Street and St Mary Street. Turn right for the pub. To see the house where Coleridge lived turn left up Lime Street.

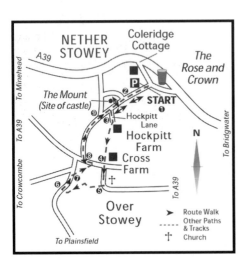

# Enmore

## A walk in parkland

## *The Tynte Arms*

**MAP:** OS EXPLORER 140 QUANTOCK HILLS (GR 242349)

**WALK 11**

**DISTANCE:** $2\frac{1}{2}$ MILES

**DIRECTIONS TO START:** ENMORE IS A SMALL VILLAGE SHELTERED BY THE EASTERN SLOPES OF THE QUANTOCK HILLS ABOUT 6 MILES WEST OF BRIDGWATER. FROM THE A39 IN BRIDGWATER TAKE THE ROAD HEADING WEST FOR DURLEIGH. PASS THE RESERVOIR AND CONTINUE FOR ABOUT 3 MILES. OUR STARTING POINT IS THE TYNTE ARMS AT ENMORE CAR PARK, WHICH YOU WILL SEE INDICATED BY THE PUB SIGN ON YOUR RIGHT. THE PUB IS A FEW YARDS FURTHER ON YOUR LEFT.
**PARKING:** IN THE PUB CAR PARK.

Enmore is one of Somerset's most remote and peaceful villages, hidden among leafy lanes with a backdrop of wooded hills. A fine church set on a ridge with views north over Bridgwater Bay to the Welsh hills overlooks a handful of attractive stone houses. Close by are the remains of a mock-medieval castle still surrounded by its park. From the pub we follow a lane to explore the village then cross the park and take field paths to enjoy a splendid view of Barford Park, an exquisite country house built during the reign of Queen Anne, which could have come straight from the pages of a Jane Austen novel. Lanes lead us back to the pub past a school with an interesting history.

## The Tynte Arms at Enmore

This is a real country pub, comfortable and welcoming, popular with locals and visitors alike. It takes its name from the Tynte family who at one time owned a great deal of land in the area. Members of the family took part in six of the eight crusades to the Holy Land, commemorated by the six shields on their coat of arms featured on the inn sign.

Once you have enjoyed the friendly atmosphere, well-kept ales and delicious food at the Tynte Arms I am sure you will wish to return. Four real ales – Champflower from Cottage, Wadworth 6X, Cotleigh Tawny and Exmoor Ale – are available along with cider and wines. A wide range of tempting dishes is on offer. Fish is a speciality and when we called the menu included Bantry Bay mussels and black bream with fresh herbs. Among other choices were sliced beef with a red wine and mushroom sauce and chicken breast filled with Brie and wrapped in smoked ham.

The inn is open from 10 am to 3 pm and from 6 pm to 11 pm every day. Meals are served throughout opening times. Overnight accommodation is also available. Telephone: 01278 671351.

## The Walk

① Turn right from the entrance to the Tynte Arms car park for a few yards then turn right up Frog Lane opposite the front of the pub. The lane leads gently uphill then curves left through the village. The churchyard – a mass of snowdrops early in the year – is on your right. As you walk up to the south doorway of the church you

*Norman dog tooth moulding surrounds the doorway of Enmore church*

pass the steps of an ancient cross. The doorway, surrounded by Norman dog tooth moulding, survives from an earlier church on this site. The beautiful west window was added in the 13th century. The two helmets on each side of the chancel arch were part of the armour of the Malet family, who were granted the manorial rights of Enmore by William the Conqueror in 1100.

As well as the superb view northwards from the churchyard there is a good view of Enmore Castle. It was built during the 18th century by the Earl of Egmont, complete with a dry moat and drawbridge. Mounting costs forced his successor to sell it to Nicholas Broadmead, who demolished all but the west wing, which remains today.

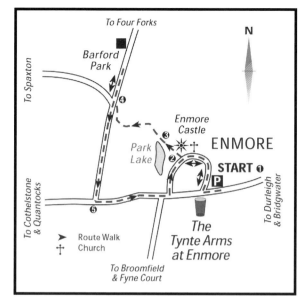

**Fyne Court** at Broomfield, 2 miles south of Enmore, has a visitor centre and offers woodland and nature trails. It is the headquarters of the Somerset Wildlife Trust. Open daily 9 am to 6 pm. Telephone: 01823 451587.

hedge on your left to walk up to a gate at the top by a footpath sign. Turn left through the gate to the lane for Four Forks.

④ Turn right along the lane for a fine view of Barford Park, built in 1710. Then retrace your steps and keep ahead along the lane for almost a mile to a T-junction.

② Just past the church you pass the brick columns either side of the drive to the castle and come to a footpath sign pointing right. Turn right, go through a gate and keep ahead over the park with a fence close on your left. Beyond the fence, parkland slopes down to the lake. When the fence turns left towards the lake keep straight on over the grass and cross a stile.

③ Keep ahead beside a field with woods on your left downhill. Look for a small iron gate at the foot of the field. Go through the gate, turn left and walk to a bridge on your right. Cross the bridge, bear left then right round the corner of a field with a

⑤ Turn left towards Enmore. Shortly you pass Enmore County Primary School. Originally known as Enmore National School, it is possible that this was the first free elementary school to be established in England, founded in 1810 by the Rev John Poole. You may of course continue down the lane to the Tynte Arms but I would suggest you turn left up School Lane and follow the lane round to the right for a last look at the church and the view before retracing your steps down Frog Lane to the pub.

# Creech St Michael

A canalside ramble

## *The Riverside Tavern*

| MAP: OS EXPLORER 128 TAUNTON AND BLACKDOWN HILLS (GR 275285) | WALK 12 | DISTANCE: 3 MILES |
|---|---|---|

**DIRECTIONS TO START:** CREECH ST MICHAEL IS ABOUT 5 MILES EAST OF TAUNTON. LEAVE THE M5 AT JUNCTION 25 ALONG THE A358 AND AFTER ABOUT $\frac{1}{4}$ MILE TURN LEFT TO DRIVE THROUGH RUISHTON TO CREECH ST MICHAEL. CROSS THE RIVER TONE AS YOU APPROACH THE VILLAGE AND BEAR RIGHT FOR ONLY A FEW YARDS THEN TURN LEFT ALONG VICARAGE LANE – YOU WILL SEE AN UNOBTRUSIVE BOAT SIGN. THE LANE CURVES LEFT TO A LARGE CANALSIDE PARKING AREA ON THE RIGHT.
**PARKING:** IN THE CANALSIDE CAR PARK.

Creech St Michael is an attractive village in the lush vale of Taunton Deane, close to the River Tone and the recently restored Bridgwater and Taunton Canal. We start with a ramble along the canal towpath, which is raised above the surrounding countryside giving wide views to the Quantock and Blackdown Hills. Wildlife abounds: mallards, moorhens and coots scuttle across the water with their families in summer, mute swans sail serenely past, kingfishers dart beneath the willows. Purple loosestrife, yellow flag irises and pink flowering rushes fringe the water's edge. After passing Charlton Manor, which dates from the 17th century, we follow field paths back to the village to visit the pub beside the river and perhaps take a stroll along the bank.

## The Riverside Tavern

Superbly situated overlooking the River Tone, the tavern has possibly welcomed guests since the 13th century! It stands beside the church and a document dated 1797 states that at one time it was known as the 'Old Church House'. Huge foundation stones suggest that in medieval days it was a monastic building where the monks would bake bread and brew beer for 'Church Ales', annual festivities which provided funds for repairs. Today there is a very much wider range of excellent home-cooked food on offer. Among the dishes when we called were chicken breast with mushrooms, onions, tomatoes and garlic in red wine, grilled swordfish with jumbo prawns and a tempting mixed grill comprising steak, gammon, sausages, fried eggs and a pork cutlet. A variety of bar snacks are also available. Real ale is Cotleigh's Tawny Bitter and there is a range of keg beers and lagers. In good weather you can enjoy attractive river views from the sunny patio.

Opening hours are from 12 noon to 3 pm and from 7 pm to 11 pm throughout the week. Food is served from 12 noon to 2 pm and from 7 pm to 9 pm every day except Monday and Sunday evening. You are asked to phone beforehand if you intend a group visit. Telephone: 01823 442257.

## The Walk

① From the car park walk up to the canal towpath and turn right with the canal on your left. The canal was completed in 1841, carrying coal and iron from South Wales to the towns of inland Somerset and

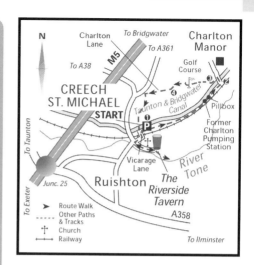

taking the county's wool and agricultural produce to Britain's urban centres. After 1866 it gradually fell into disuse, superseded by the railway.

Continue past a small bridge. After about $\frac{1}{2}$ mile you pass a large brick building. This was originally Charlton Engine House, built in 1826 to pump water from the River Tone (300 yards away) into the canal. It once housed two pumps powered by a steam-operated beam engine. Later the pumps supplied water to replenish steam locomotives on their non-stop run between Paddington and Penzance. The pillbox close by is a reminder that during the Second World War the canal was an important part of the Wessex Stop Line, intended to halt the westward progress of the German armies should they invade.

② Turn left over brick-built Charlton Bridge. L-shaped Charlton Manor is on your right. Walk up the lane past the entrance to Lashpool Farm. After about 50 yards turn left over a stile along a wide grassy track.

*The towpath beside the Bridgwater and Taunton Canal makes a delightful walk*

③ In another 50 yards go through a gate on your right to a golf course. Follow the signed path over the green, keeping a hedge close on your left. The path turns right with a fence on your right. Continue for about 30 yards then turn left over a stile. Keep straight ahead over a field to the corner of a hedge, then follow the path as it bears very slightly left to lead you over a stile into Charlton Lane.

④ Follow the lane as it runs between houses. Ignore the first footpath sign on the left and continue along the lane. Just past a telephone box turn left, over a stile, and follow the broad track ahead for about 30 yards. Continue along the narrow path beside a field with a hedge on your right. Cross a stile and keep ahead with the hedge now on your left. The path curves right then shortly left over a stile. Keep straight ahead over fields and wooden footbridges to cross a final stile on your right. A path past houses leads you over a canal bridge to your car park.

Walk or drive back down Vicarage Lane and turn left for the Riverside Tavern. The 13th century church close by is noted for its fine wagon roof. The yew tree outside the porch is reputed to be a thousand years old and shelters the village stocks.

# Corfe

## A Somerset panorama
# *The White Hart Inn*

**MAP:** OS EXPLORER 128 TAUNTON AND BLACKDOWN HILLS (GR 233198)

**WALK 13**

**DISTANCE:** 2$\frac{1}{2}$ MILES

**DIRECTIONS TO START:** CORFE IS A SMALL VILLAGE 3 MILES SOUTH OF TAUNTON. IT LIES BESIDE THE B3170, WHICH RUNS SOUTH FROM TAUNTON TO MEET THE A303. **PARKING:** IN THE PARKING AREA IN MILL LANE BESIDE THE NORTH WALL OF THE CHURCH. TURN BY THE WAR MEMORIAL AND THE PARKING AREA IS ON YOUR RIGHT.

You must choose a fine day for this walk as your reward for a short climb through oak and beech woods is a magnificent view over nearly all the plains and hills of Somerset! We start from Corfe, an attractive village on the southern fringe of the cream and cider country of Taunton Deane. Just south of the village rise the thickly wooded slopes of the Blackdown Hills and we follow a sunken track into the hills to enjoy this stunning view before returning to the village along a quiet lane.

## The White Hart Inn

The White Hart describes itself as 'the Country Inn you'll be comfortable in' and I think you will find this friendly pub amply fulfils this promise. The lounge and bar areas are traditionally furnished with polished wood and there is a separate dining room. A wide choice of snacks is on offer. Knowledgeable customers recommend the steak baguettes! Full meals, when we called, included the White Hart's own steak, kidney and real ale pie, loin pork chop with whole grain mustard and cream sauce and bacon wrapped chicken in Stilton sauce.

Real ales are Marston's Pedigree, Cotleigh's Wiveliscombe Barn Owl and Flowers IPA. A good choice of wines and ciders is also available.

Opening times are from 12 noon to 3 pm and from 5.30 pm to 11 pm; on Saturdays the pub is open all day from 12 noon. Food is served from 12 noon to 2 pm and from 7 pm to 9 pm. Telephone: 01823 421388.

## The Walk

① From the parking area walk past the war memorial to return to the main road. Turn left to pass the church on your left. The church of St Nicholas stands in an idyllic spot overlooking the valley of the Broughton Brook. It was largely rebuilt in 1842 but has preserved its original Norman font with finely carved interlocking arches. Some of the thatched houses and cottages set beside grassy lawns near the church date from the 16th century. Pass the lane to Pitminster and the White Hart pub on your right and continue along the footway.

② Turn right to walk up Adcombe Lane. This was once the main road to Honiton! Now all is peace as the traffic takes the B3170 along the valley below you.

③ Just past Adcombe Cottage turn right up the next drive on the right. On the other side of the road a fingerpost indicates this bridleway. Continue past a house on the left and go through a gate. The path leads through another gate and becomes a sunken stony track winding uphill through some of the fine woodlands characteristic of the Blackdowns. Limestone was quarried in the hills, and these dense woods provided fuel for the kilns which burnt the lime for agricultural purposes. The track widens as you near the top of the hill and crosses a field to take you through a gate and meet Adcombe Lane.

④ Pause here and look back. From this splendid vantage point you can see all the Somerset hills. You look east over the Levels to the Polden ridge and the Mendips, north over the Vale of Taunton

*Adcombe Lane leads to the wooded Blackdown Hills*

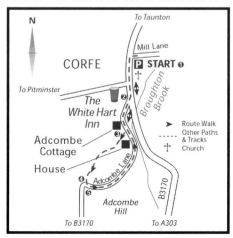

Deane to the Quantocks and west to the Brendons to catch just a glimpse of Exmoor.

⑤ With your back to the gate turn left to walk along Adcombe Lane, which follows a high ridge at this point, giving more wide-ranging views. The lane gradually descends into the valley to pass the bridleway we took at point 3. Retrace your steps along the lane to the B3170, turning left to walk back through the village to the White Hart and your car.

# North Curry
## The magic of the Levels
### *The Bird in Hand*

**MAP:** OS EXPLORER 128 TAUNTON AND BLACKDOWN HILLS (GR 319254)

**WALK 14**

**DISTANCE:** 2½ MILES

**DIRECTIONS TO START:** NORTH CURRY IS ABOUT 6 MILES EAST OF TAUNTON, 2 MILES NORTH OF THE A378 LANGPORT ROAD. FROM THE M5 LEAVE AT JUNCTION 25, TAKING THE A358 ILMINSTER ROAD. TURN EAST AT THORNFALCON TRAFFIC LIGHTS ALONG THE A378 AND AFTER ABOUT ¼ MILE TURN LEFT, HEADING NORTH-EAST FOR NORTH CURRY. **PARKING:** JUST PAST THE BIRD IN HAND TURN LEFT INTO QUEEN SQUARE. AT THE ROAD JUNCTION TURN SHARP RIGHT (WAR MEMORIAL ON YOUR LEFT) ALONG THE UNSIGNED ROAD, CHURCH STREET. WHERE CHURCH STREET BEGINS TO CURVE RIGHT, SIGNED 'THE FOSSE', PARK ON THE LEFT BESIDE THE CHURCHYARD WALL.

The lush, well-watered grasslands of the Somerset Levels, which provided early harvests of hay and rich pasture for cattle, gave the county its name 'the land of the Summer people'. In the past much of the land lay under water in winter and many areas still flood today. But this unique landscape is home for a wealth of birdlife including herons, lapwings, snipe and mute swans. Water-loving plants, such as yellow flag iris, flowering rush and arrowhead, flourish beside the innumerable drainage ditches or rhynes. This short stroll leads from North Curry, a historic village designated a conservation area, across Curry Moor to the banks of the River Tone.

## The Bird in Hand

The Bird in Hand is a traditional, inviting village inn with flagstoned floors, beamed ceilings and inglenook fireplaces. The large bar area is furnished with wooden settles and benches and old yew tables. There is a separate, tastefully decorated restaurant. An imaginative range of home-cooked food is on offer including vegetarian, Continental and English dishes. When we called, bar food included baguettes with a wide variety of fillings, among them fillet steak with onions and mushrooms. Featured on the 'Specials' board were the pub's award-winning pork, bacon and black pudding sausages, whole bass, and salmon fillet with chive sauce. There is a special menu for children. A carvery is served at lunchtime on Sunday (book in advance for this). Real ales are Badger Tanglefoot, Butcombe Gold and Otter Ale.

Lunchtime opening Monday to Friday and on Sunday is from 12 noon to 3 pm, on Saturday from 12 noon to 4 pm. In the evenings the pub is open from 6 pm to 11 pm Monday to Thursday and Saturday, 5.30 pm to 11 pm on Friday, and 7 pm to 10.30 pm on Sunday. Meals are served every day from 12 noon to 2 pm and from 7 pm to 9.30 pm (except Monday at present, but this may change – ring for details). Telephone: 01823 490248.

## The Walk

① With the church wall on your left, go through the small wooden gate into the churchyard. The church of St Peter and St Paul, with its central octagonal tower and finely vaulted south porch, is known as

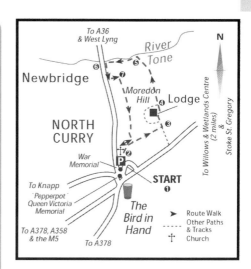

'The Cathedral of the Moors'. It is sited on the crest of the ridge with views northwards over the Levels. When the narrow path divides bear a little right and keep ahead to pass the church on your left. Walk down the churchyard to a small iron gate.

② Go through the gate, keep ahead for a few yards then bear right downhill to a hedge. Follow the path with the hedge on your left. Keep straight on past a footpath sign on your left. Cross a stile and follow the path up Moredon Hill. As you near the top of the hill, go over a stile by a gate. The path drops a little to another stile by a gate.

③ Cross the stile to a lane, turn left and follow the lane until you see large iron gates ahead and a small lodge on your right. Bear right to walk round the side of the lodge, keeping it on your left, to a wide gravel track.

④ Cross a stile by a gate and follow the sunken track as it drops steeply downhill.

*North Curry church is known as the Cathedral of the Moors*

At the foot of the hill the gravel gives way to a grassy embanked droveway running between rhynes. Follow this across Curry Moor. A bridge leads you over a rhyne. Go through a gate and make your way over the grass ahead, bearing a little left to the raised bank of the River Tone. Beyond the ridge on your right lies the island of Athelney, where, in AD 878, Alfred took refuge from the Danes. Etched against the horizon to the north-east you will see Glastonbury Tor.

⑤ Turn left beside the river as far as the road at New Bridge.

⑥ Turn left beside the road for about 300 yards then turn left again, following the footpath sign along a raised track for about 150 yards.

⑦ Turn right through a gate and keep ahead with a rhyne close on your right. Cross a wooden footbridge and keep ahead beside the rhyne to cross another footbridge. Continue on the same heading over a third footbridge. There may be no clear path across the field ahead so bear right for a few yards then bear left to walk beside the field with a rhyne on your right. Cross a stile to rejoin your outbound route. Turn right to retrace your steps past the church to return to your car.

### PLACES OF INTEREST NEARBY

**Willows and Wetlands Centre**, Stoke St Gregory. Willows (or 'withies') for making baskets and furniture have been grown near North Curry for centuries. The Centre gives a fascinating insight into the craft. It offers guided tours and there is a tea room and shop. Open Monday to Saturday, 9 am to 5 pm. Telephone: 01823 490249.

# Muchelney
## The Abbey of the Levels
## *The Almonry Gallery Restaurant and Stable Tea Room*

| MAP: OS EXPLORER 129 YEOVIL AND SHERBORNE (GR 429249) | WALK 15 | DISTANCE: 3 MILES |
|---|---|---|

**DIRECTIONS TO START:** MUCHELNEY IS A SMALL VILLAGE IN THE LEVELS A MILE SOUTH OF LANGPORT. THE BEST APPROACH IS VIA THE A372. TURN FOR MUCHELNEY OPPOSITE THE CHURCH IN HUISH EPISCOPI. AFTER ABOUT 50 YARDS TURN LEFT, FOLLOWING THE SIGN FOR MUCHELNEY DOWN THE NARROW LANE LEADING TO THE VILLAGE. **PARKING:** IN THE NATIONAL TRUST CAR PARK OPEN FROM APRIL TO SEPTEMBER. TURN LEFT IN FRONT OF THE CHURCH TO THE CAR PARK ON THE RIGHT. AT OTHER TIMES PARK BESIDE THE CHURCH WALL.

The heart of Somerset is a vast plain of rich grassland, watered by slow, meandering rivers and drained by a network of ditches called rhynes. Areas of higher ground rise from this mysterious wetland, forming low islands settled by small isolated communities. One of the most historic and least changed of the villages of the Levels is Muchelney, 'the great island'. This walk visits the remains of a Benedictine abbey founded here in the 9th century, the church close by built by the monks for the villagers and the Priest's House, a late medieval house with an open-roofed hall. From Muchelney we take a short stroll beside the River Parrett and back again to enjoy wide views over the Levels and the rich variety of wildlife.

## The Almonry Gallery Restaurant and Stable Tea Room

Benedictine monks had a special duty to welcome travellers, the poor and the sick. They were cared for in the Almonry buildings opposite the abbey. After the Dissolution of the Monasteries these buildings, like most of the abbey, fell into disrepair or became barns. Today a 16th century barn, once part of the abbey guest quarters, has been renovated and is now a fully licensed restaurant serving an imaginative range of dishes. A speciality is farmhouse cheddar produced in the traditional way.

Lunch is served from 12 am to 2.30 pm and dinner from 7 pm to 9 pm, Monday to Saturday; on Sunday a roast lunch is available from 12.30 pm to 2.30 pm. The restaurant is closed on Sunday evenings, Mondays (except bank holidays) and Tuesdays.

If you fancy a baguette or a salad, or a delicious tea with home-made cakes, try the Stable Tea Room (also licensed), which is housed in the same group of buildings. Among the delights on offer are pastries with comb honey and clotted cream. Savouries include platters of smoked trout and salmon. Both the restaurant and the tea room are open from Easter to the end of October. Telephone: 01458 252560.

For the winter months, there is a country pub in Drayton which serves real ales and traditional home cooking. Telephone: 01458 250233.

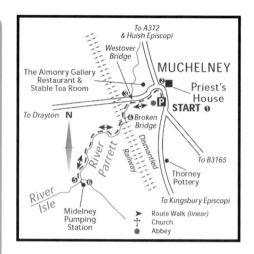

## The Walk

① Begin this walk with a visit to Muchelney Abbey. Although only the foundations of the abbey church remain, the gabled Abbot's lodging has survived. Above the kitchen and hall the five hundred year old staircase leads to the Abbot's parlour. Part of the north wall of the refectory and a few bays of the south cloister with its delicately carved upper storey have also survived. As you walk round the remains of this great building it is easy to imagine what a magnet it must have been for travellers making their way through the surrounding swamps and marshes.

The 15th century church has a wagon roof decorated with angels, so often a feature of Somerset churches. But these, in their low-cut Tudor costumes, are distinctly feminine! On either side of the north porch are two grotesque heads. Unlike gargoyles, they serve no useful purpose. Known as 'hunky punks', they are typical of this part of Somerset.

The Priest's House opposite the church can also be visited. For details see 'Places of Interest Nearby'.

*A picnic beside the River Parrett at Muchelney*

② With the church on your left bear left beside the church wall, following the lane signed for Drayton. You pass the Almonry restaurant and tea room on your right. Follow the lane as it curves right and brings you to Westover Bridge.

③ Cross the bridge and turn left over a stile to take the footpath signed for Thorney Bridge. The path is embanked and overlooks the River Parrett on your left and the flat fenland on your right. In early spring wading birds such as lapwings, snipe and curlews nest in the damp grassland, which is colourful with wild flowers – among them pink and white lady's smock and marsh marigolds. Summer brings many other meadow flowers which attract butterflies including marbled whites and hedge browns. At all times of the year you should see herons, perhaps the turquoise flash of a kingfisher, rare birds of prey and deer. I was told also that otters have returned to the river.

④ At the broken down railway bridge turn right with the river still on your left, cross a stile and continue along the river bank for about a mile.

⑤ Follow the path round to the left, cross the river and bear left again to see Midelney Pumping Station. Built in 1963 the station regulates water levels on the surrounding moors to provide the right conditions for wildlife.

⑥ Retrace your route beside the river, turning right over Westover Bridge to return to Muchelney.

### PLACES OF INTEREST NEARBY

**Muchelney Abbey** (English Heritage) is open from April to October, daily from 10 am to 6 pm (5 pm in October). Telephone: 01458 250664.

**The Priest's House** (NT) is open from the beginning of April to the end of September, Sunday and Monday 2 pm to 5 pm. Telephone: 01458 252621.

**Muchelney Pottery** is a mile south of the village, at Thorney. The shop is open all year: Monday to Friday, 9 am to 1 pm and 2 pm to 5 pm, Saturday 9 am to 1 pm. Telephone: 01458 250324.

# Barrington
## A golden village and an Elizabethan manor
# *The Royal Oak*

**MAP:** OS EXPLORER 128 TAUNTON AND BLACKDOWN HILLS (GR 389182)

**WALK 16**

**DISTANCE:** 3 MILES

**DIRECTIONS TO START:** BARRINGTON IS A SMALL VILLAGE ABOUT 6 MILES NORTH-EAST OF ILMINSTER. THE BEST APPROACH IS VIA THE B3168 HEADING NORTH FROM ILMINSTER. THE VILLAGE IS ALSO SIGNED OFF THE A358 TAUNTON TO ILMINSTER ROAD. APPROACHING VIA THE A303 FOLLOW THE SIGNS FOR BARRINGTON COURT. **PARKING:** PATRONS CAN LEAVE CARS – PARKED TIDILY – IN THE ROYAL OAK CAR PARK. OR THERE IS ROOM TO PARK OPPOSITE THE PUB BY THE CHURCHYARD WALL.

Barrington lies among the tumbled hills forming Somerset's border with Dorset. Houses and cottages built of golden stone from Ham Hill cluster around the church of the Blessed Virgin Mary, which dates from the 13th century and has a splendid octagonal tower. East of the village a medieval manor was replaced in the 16th century by Barrington Court, an elegant stately home surrounded by formal gardens designed by Gertrude Jekyll, now owned by the National Trust. From Barrington the walk follows quiet country lanes to visit two more charming villages before returning over the fields with fine views north over the Levels.

## The Royal Oak

This popular pub stands in the heart of the village opposite the church and offers a warm and cheerful welcome to all comers. The attractive old world bar and dining area are furnished with solid dark oak tables and comfortable cushioned chairs. Proceedings are supervised by the pub ghost, a little old lady with a quiet disposition, called Janet. She must have told them her name!

Real ales are Butcombe, Young's Special and Fuller's London Pride. In addition there are guest ales and a wide choice of wines. When we called, the menu included creamy fish and prawn pie, duck and cherry pie and prawn longboats with salad. The pub, which is dog and child friendly, is open all day on Saturday from 11.30 am to 11 pm. On Sunday the hours are from 12 noon to 10.30 pm and on Monday from 5 pm to 11 pm. The rest of the week opening hours are from 12 noon to 3 pm and from 5 pm to 11 pm. Apart from Monday, lunchtime food is served from 12 noon to 2.15 pm and from 6 pm to 9.30 pm. Telephone: 01460 53455.

## The Walk

① Turn right from the front door of the pub to pass the church on your left.

② Just past the church turn left up Copse Shute Lane and keep straight on past a footpath sign on the right along a tree-shaded path. After about 30 yards turn right, following the signs up some steps to cross a stile into a field. Bear half-right up the field to cross another stile. Keep ahead beside the next field with a hedge

on your right. At the top of the field bear right to a lane.

③ Turn left to follow the lane to a T-junction. Cross straight over to take the narrow path ahead signed for Stocklinch and Pound Lane. The path curves right then after about 60 yards swings left to meet Stoney Lane in another golden stone village, Stocklinch St Magdalen. Turn right to walk past a row of deep-thatched houses, which are lost in flowers in summertime, to a junction.

④ Turn left along Owl Street, which leads through Stocklinch Ottersey. The lane curves left.

---

### PLACES OF INTEREST NEARBY

A visit to **Barrington Court** and its beautiful gardens can easily be combined with this walk. The gardens, house, restaurant and shop are open daily (except Wednesday) from April to September, 11 am to 5.30 pm, and from Thursday to Sunday in March and October, from 11 am to 4.30 pm. Telephone: 01460 241938.

*Stocklinch St Magdalen*

⑤ Just past the village hall on the right, turn left through a small wooden gate with a footpath sign for Stoney Lane to walk up to the church of St Mary Magdalen. This tiny church is a delight, with an outside staircase giving access to an 18th century gallery and a bellcote for three bells worked by wheels.

The present footpaths now differ slightly from the OS map. Follow the grassy path ahead, passing the church on your right. Leave the churchyard down some steps and cross a stile to a field. Keep ahead across the field to go through a wide gap in a hedge. The path may not be defined at this point but walk up the next field, bearing a little left to a gate in the left hand corner of the opposite hedge. Go through the gate and follow the wide track ahead to Stoney Lane.

⑥ Turn right up the lane, which swings left to meet another lane. Bear left for about 50 yards to a T-junction.

⑦ Turn right to follow this sunken lane for about $^1/_4$ mile to a footpath indicated by a post alongside a stile on the left.

⑧ Cross the stile into a field and keep ahead with a hedge then a fence on your right. Follow the fence round to the right to cross a stile. A footpath sign directs you down a grassy path with a wood on your right and a fence on your left. Cross stiles either side of a track and continue down a grassy path between high hedges. This soon becomes a lane and joins the main street in Barrington. Turn left to return to the Royal Oak and your car.

# Dowlish Wake

## In Somerset's cider country

## *The New Inn*

**MAP:** OS EXPLORER 128 TAUNTON AND BLACKDOWN HILLS (GR 375124)

**WALK 17**

**DISTANCE:** 2½ MILES

**DIRECTIONS TO START:** DOWLISH WAKE IS A SMALL VILLAGE ABOUT 2 MILES SOUTH-EAST OF ILMINSTER. THE BEST APPROACH IS VIA THE A303. LEAVE THE A303 ALONG THE A358, HEADING SOUTH TOWARDS CHARD. DRIVE THROUGH DONYATT AND AFTER ABOUT A MILE TURN LEFT, FOLLOWING THE SIGN FOR KINGSTONE. IN KINGSTONE TURN RIGHT FOR DOWLISH WAKE. DRIVE THROUGH THE VILLAGE, PASSING THE CHURCH AND CIDER MILLS ON YOUR RIGHT, TO A FORK. TURN LEFT, SIGNED 'CUDWORTH' AND THE NEW INN IS A FEW YARDS FURTHER ON YOUR RIGHT. DOWLISH WAKE IS ALSO SIGNED FROM THE A30. **PARKING:** PATRONS CAN LEAVE THEIR CARS IN THE PUB CAR PARK OPPOSITE THE PUB.

Dowlish Wake, built of golden Ham Hill stone, is one of Somerset's most beautiful villages. The main street is threaded by a stream and bordered by a footpath which you reach over tiny bridges. A packhorse bridge stands beside the ford. The village lies in lush country-side stretching east from the slopes of the Blackdowns, surrounded by gently undulating hills. This area of Somerset is noted for its cider made by traditional methods from locally grown apples and some of the finest comes from Perry's Cider Mills in the heart of the village.

## The New Inn

This is a warm-hearted, traditional pub, the focal point of village life. The beamed bar is comfortably furnished with sturdy wooden tables and chairs, and a wood burning stove stands in the huge inglenook fireplace. You can take part in typical pub games such as shove ha'penny, bar billiards and table skittles and families have a separate room with a pleasant outlook over the garden. The pub is decorated with racing pictures and mementoes and a collection of pub jugs bearing different brand names.

Real ales are Butcombe Bitter, Wadworth 6X and Otter Ale. When we called, a tempting menu included chicken breast with a creamy Stilton or Cheddar sauce, sliced lamb's liver with bacon, mushrooms and onions cooked in red wine, and an all-day breakfast. There is also a wide range of bar snacks.

Opening times Monday to Saturday are from 11 am to 3 pm and from 6.30 pm to 11 pm; Sundays from 12 noon to 3 pm and from 7 pm to 10.30 pm. Meals are served from 12 noon to 2 pm and from 7 pm to 9 pm. Telephone: 01460 52413.

## The Walk

① Leave the pub entrance and turn left to the junction with the main street. Turn right to take the footpath beside the stream. Walk past the lane to the Cider Mills and the packhorse bridge on your left to a T-junction. Facing the junction is the Dower House, dated 1674, once occupied by ladies of the Speke family. The Spekes inherited the lordship of the

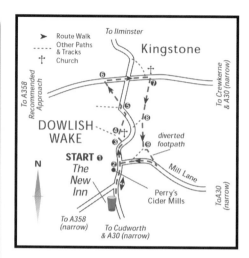

manor in 1420 and held it for nearly five hundred years.

② Turn left, signed for Kingstone, and follow the raised footpath uphill to the church. The 15th century Chantry Chapel houses a Ham stone effigy of Isabel Wake, who died in 1359, and the tomb of John Hanning Speke, the Victorian explorer who travelled 2,500 miles across Africa to confirm Lake Victoria as the source of the Nile.

③ With the church on your right follow the churchyard wall past the parking area on your left to face a small stone building. Until 1949 it was the school, now it serves as the village hall.

④ Cross the stile on your left, signed for Moolham. Do not follow the obvious path ahead leading across the field (we are not going to Moolham!) but turn immediately right to walk beside the field to rejoin the road to Kingstone.

⑤ Turn left for about 30 yards. Cross a joining tarmac track on your left and then

*The path by the stream in Dowlish Wake*

turnpike house stands in a commanding position on the corner. Following the sign for Crewkerne, walk through the village as far as the church.

⑦ Turn right along the footpath opposite the church, signed to Mill Lane and Dowlish Wake. The path now leads slightly downhill over a long field well known for ammonites; we found several half-buried in the path. Many millions of years ago Kingstone lay under a shallow warm sea teeming with creatures who have left these fossilised remains.

⑧ Keep ahead past a footpath to Dowlish Wake on your right to descend some steps, cross a gully and a stile and continue down another field. At the foot of the field you pass a barn on your right and meet a hedge. There is a track on your right leading down to Mill Lane but this is private. So turn left with the hedge on your right to the corner of the hedge.

⑨ The right-of-way has been diverted at this point. From the corner of the hedge bear half-right down the field towards a large oak tree to join Mill Lane. Turn right along Mill Lane to the junction with the Kingstone road and turn left to retrace your steps past the packhorse bridge, then bear left, following the sign for Cudworth, to the New Inn.

turn left along a narrow path through the hedge and follow the field path to meet the road just west of Kingstone village.

⑥ Turn right for Kingstone, passing the turning for Dowlish Wake. Continue to the junction with the Ilminster road. A

---

**PLACES OF INTEREST NEARBY**

**Perry's Cider Mills.** Discover how the best cider, including the award-winning Redstreak, is made, sample before you buy and visit the rural life museum. Entry is free. The mills are open every day (except Christmas and New Year) on weekdays from 9 am to 5.30 pm, Saturdays 9.30 am to 4.30 pm, Sundays 10 am to 1 pm. Telephone: 01460 52681.

---

# Winsham

## The setting for 'To the Manor Born'

# *The Bell Inn*

**MAP:** OS EXPLORER 29 LYME REGIS AND BRIDPORT (GR 376064)

**WALK 18**

**DISTANCE:** 2½ MILES

**DIRECTIONS TO START:** WINSHAM VILLAGE IS ABOUT 5 MILES SOUTH-EAST OF CHARD. TURN FOR WINSHAM OFF THE A30 ALONG THE B3167. CONTINUE FOR ABOUT 2 MILES, TURN LEFT IN STREET ALONG THE B3162 TO DRIVE THROUGH WHATLEY TO WINSHAM. PASS THE CROSS ON YOUR LEFT AND KEEP STRAIGHT ON DOWN CHURCH STREET AS FAR AS THE BELL INN ON YOUR LEFT. **PARKING:** PATRONS MAY USE THE PUB CAR PARK. ALTERNATIVELY THERE IS GOOD ROADSIDE PARKING CLOSE BY.

Winsham is a friendly, thriving village in the valley of the Axe close to the border with Dorset. Fine buildings include the 13th century church, its central tower graced with a rare painting of the crucifixion, the school, dated 1850, and the Jubilee Hall, given by Lord Bridport, formerly Lord of the Manor of nearby Cricket St Thomas, to mark Queen Victoria's Jubilee. In 1685 the ill-fated Duke of Monmouth marched his pitchfork-carrying troops up Church Street and on to Windwhistle Hill prior to the Battle of Sedgemoor. This walk follows part of his route and takes a beautiful path through the Cricket St Thomas valley, the setting for the television comedy *To the Manor Born*. A short detour reveals the small lodge which the heroine, Audrey, makes her home, having sold the manor for lack of funds.

## The Bell Inn

The Bell is a genuine country pub offering a warm and friendly welcome to all comers. It provides the venue for many events in this lively village. These include skittle evenings, quiz nights, parties, small drama productions and music nights indoors and out, many for charities. You may quickly find yourself drawn into the fun! The cosy bar area has blazing log fires in winter. The walls are decorated with delightful coloured prints of local village scenes, the work of Michael Cooper, who lives in Street.

Home-made pies are a Bell speciality. Among a wide choice we noted game, steak and Stilton and chicken and leek pies. Traditional 'Bubble and Squeak' also appeared on the menu. Real ales are Crop Circle, The Newcomer, Branoc and Spitfire. Cider and wines are also available.

Opening times are 12 noon to 2.30 pm and 7 pm to 11 pm, Monday to Friday, 12 noon to 3 pm and 7 pm to 11 pm on Saturday, 12 noon to 3 pm and 7 pm to 10.30 pm on Sunday. Food is served from 12 noon to 2 pm and 7 pm to 9 pm except on Sunday evenings. Telephone: 01460 30677.

## The Walk

① Turn right from the front door of the Bell to walk up Church Street towards the old market cross at the point where five roads meet. On your right you will see Back Street and Fore Street. Turn right to walk up Back Street past pretty colour-

### PLACES OF INTEREST NEARBY

**The Wildlife Park** at Cricket St Thomas, just north of Winsham, contains over 500 animals, including many endangered species, in picturesque surroundings. The safari train is popular, and a café and restaurant offer refreshments. Cricket House is the 'Grantleigh Manor' of *To the Manor Born*. The Wildlife Park is open every day except Christmas Day, 10 am to 6 pm or dusk in winter (last admission 4 pm). Guide dogs only in the park. Telephone: 01460 30111.

**Forde Abbey** (actually in Dorset, but just southwest of Winsham) is a fascinating 15th to 17th century house surrounded by gardens. Café. Open April to October, 1 pm to 4.30 pm, Sundays, Wednesdays and bank holidays. Telephone: 01460 220231.

**Hornsbury Mill**, on the A358 between Chard and Donyatt, is a 200 year old working water mill with landscaped gardens and a restaurant. Open every day, 10 am to 4.30 pm, 6.30 pm to 11 pm. Telephone: 01460 63317.

washed cottages to a T-junction. This is High Street.

② Bear left to follow Limekiln Lane, which runs uphill then drops into a wooded valley threaded by the Cricket St Thomas stream. Cross the footbridge over the stream and pass a house on the left.

③ A few yards past the house turn left (no sign) through the pine trees. Cross a cattle grid and follow the path ahead, known as The Chalkway, as it winds through the valley. This tranquil valley was chosen as the setting for *To the Manor Born*. In his fascinating book *The Winsham I Remember* (which is available at the post office), W.H. Paull remarks that the valley 'has always been a romantic spot,

*Audrey's lodge in 'To the Manor Born'*

and for years the song of the nightingale drew people from the village just to listen'.

④ When The Chalkway meets Colham Lane we turn left but to see the lodge used in the comedy make a short detour and keep straight ahead. Follow the lane for about ¼ mile to the lodge on the right beside a drive to the manor. Retrace your steps and turn right down Colham Lane. This attractive narrow lane was once the main road out of Winsham and the route taken by Monmouth during the 1685 rebellion. Turn right when you reach Back Lane once more then turn left down Church Street to return to your car.

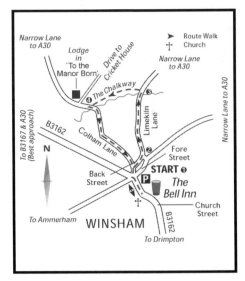

# Compton Dundon
## A magnificent viewpoint in the Polden Hills
### *The Castlebrook Inn*

**MAP:** OS EXPLORER 4 MENDIP HILLS WEST (GR 490327)

**WALK 19**

**DISTANCE:** 3 MILES

**DIRECTIONS TO START:** COMPTON DUNDON IS A SMALL VILLAGE BESIDE THE B3151, MIDWAY BETWEEN SOMERTON AND STREET. THE CASTLEBROOK INN IS AT THE SOUTH END OF THE VILLAGE. **PARKING:** THE INN CAR PARK.

Compton Dundon is set in a glorious landscape of low wooded hills at the eastern end of the Polden ridge. It is really two villages. Compton lies in a valley at the foot of Butleigh Wood in the shadow of two cone-shaped hills west of the village. Tiny Dundon is tucked neatly into a valley between them. This walk takes you past thickly-wooded Dundon Hill to climb the open grassy slopes of Lollover Hill and enjoy one of the most spectacular views in Somerset. So choose a clear day for this walk and take your binoculars as this remote area is rich in wildlife, including deer and badgers.

## The Castlebrook Inn

You step back into the past as you enter this historic inn. It was built around 1550 as an open-hall house and retains its high timbered and wattled roof. Now, this is concealed by low ceilings crossed by massive beams but in the bar area you will find a real reminder of times past – a magnificent inglenook fireplace with benches either side of the hearth. Mind your head on the huge cross-beam if you are tempted to sit here!

The pub offers a warm welcome and excellent home-cooked food. As well as favourites such as cottage pie made to their own recipe and sausage and mash served with peas and rich gravy, the menu includes panfried horseshoe gammon served with egg or pineapple, mushrooms and onion rings, poachers' chicken – breast of chicken wrapped in bacon, topped with cheese and coated with barbecue sauce – and a roast of the day. Three real ales are always available.

In summer the inn is open all day. At other times opening times are 12 noon to 3 pm and 6 pm to 11 pm. Food is served from 12 noon to 2 pm and from 7 pm to 9 pm. Overnight accommodation is also available. Telephone: 01458 443632.

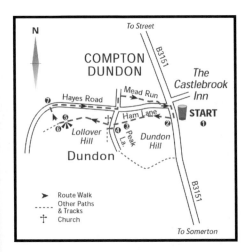

## The Walk

① Turn left from the car park entrance and walk beside the B3151 for about 30 yards to a stile leading into a field on the right.

② Cross the stile and small plank bridge and continue up the field ahead with a hedge on your right. Beyond the wooded slopes of Dundon Hill on your left you will see Lollover Hill scored with strip lynchets, the result of the desperate need for land in the 13th century. Cross the next stile and walk up the field, gaining height. The long ridge of the Polden Hills stretches northwards to the sea on your right. The monument rising above the woods commemorates Vice-Admiral Sir Samuel Hood of nearby Butleigh Wootton.

Cross another stile and keep ahead, with the hedge still on your right, to go through a gap in the opposite hedge. Pass a small wooden gate on your right. Continue uphill and go through a gate to a track.

③ The track becomes an asphalt lane and leads past Dundon School and some attractive thatched houses to a T-junction, Peak Lane. Bear left for about 30 yards then turn right, following the footpath sign for Lollover Hill.

④ Go up the steps and follow a narrow

*Descending Lollover Hill*

path up more steps to a crosspath. Turn right and follow the path as it curves left and becomes a broad track winding up the hillside. As you near the top of the hill cross a stile and keep straight on with a fence on your right. After crossing the next stile the path bears left to lead you over another stile near the highest point on Lollover Hill and reveal the wonderful view I promised. You look north and west far over King's Sedgemoor, the site of the Duke of Monmouth's defeat in 1685, to Bridgwater Bay. Due west lies Athelney where Alfred sought refuge from the Danes and planned to regain his kingdom. Beyond Athelney rise the Quantock Hills.

⑤ Follow the path downhill for about ¼ mile and look for a double plank bridge and stile on your right.

⑥ Turn right over the stile and bridge and walk downhill towards a house with a hedge on your right. Cross a stile and continue to join Hayes Road.

⑦ Turn right and follow this lane along the valley to a crossroads. You can of course keep straight on along Ham Lane to meet the B3151 in Compton Dundon but in dry weather I would suggest you take a more interesting route and turn left at the crossroads along Hurst Drove. Pass a turning on the left and continue to a footpath sign. Turn right as the sign directs along Mead Run, which follows the bank of a rhyne and brings you to Ham Lane. Bear left to the B3151 and turn right to walk through Compton Dundon back to your car.

## PLACES OF INTEREST NEARBY

**Glastonbury,** famous for its Abbey and Tor, is within easy reach via the A39 north of Street. In Street, **Clark's Shoe Museum** documents the history of the firm and the story of shoes with examples of footwear from earliest times. Open daily, Monday to Friday 10 am to 4.45 pm, Saturday to 6 pm, Sunday 12 noon to 6 pm. Telephone: 01458 43131. You can also shop for bargains in **Clark's Factory Village**. There are picnic and play areas and a café.

# Meare

## An ancient settlement on the peat moors

# *The Countryman Inn and Squires Restaurant*

**MAP:** OS EXPLORER 4 MENDIP HILLS WEST (GR 447416)

**WALK 20**

**DISTANCE:** 2 MILES

**DIRECTIONS TO START:** MEARE IS A SMALL VILLAGE BESIDE THE B3151 ABOUT 3½ MILES NORTH-WEST OF GLASTONBURY. THE COUNTRYMAN INN FACES THE ROAD. **PARKING:** THE INN CAR PARK (PLEASE ASK BEFORE LEAVING YOUR CAR WHILE YOU WALK).

Meare is built along the crest of a low ridge overlooking the wide expanse of flat peat moors lying between the southern slopes of the Mendips and the Polden Hills. In 1973 the Sweet Track, a footpath constructed of hewn timbers around 4000 BC, was discovered nearby. Until the mid 18th century when the land was drained, the village stood beside Meare Pool, a large lake 5 miles in circumference, and traces of Iron Age villages have been found on its shore. The lake became a useful source of fish for Glastonbury Abbey and the 14th century Abbot's Fish House still stands at the eastern end of the village. The old manor house beside the church, now a farm, was built as a summer retreat for the Abbot. The walk explores the village then follows footpaths beside the River Bure through lush meadows and apple orchards.

## The Countryman Inn and Squires Restaurant

The Countryman is a warm-hearted traditional country inn. There are two spacious bars, a dining area and a well-appointed restaurant. Friendly smiles greet you as you step through the door and it comes as no surprise that the pub is the centre of village life. Every year two clubs – the Masqueraders and the under sixteens known as the Keykids – meet here to plan their floats for the famous Bridgwater Carnival.

Real ales are Wadworth 6X and Fuller's London Pride and I would recommend you try the cider. It is made by a local farmer and will give you a real taste of Somerset! There is a wide range of meals on offer. These included, when we called, minted lamb steaks, and half a roast pheasant with wild mushrooms. When possible, in-gredients are locally sourced.

Opening times Monday to Saturday are from 11 am to 2.30 pm and from 7 pm to 11 pm; Sundays 12 noon to 2.30 pm and 7 pm to 10.30 pm. Food is served from 12 noon to 2.30 pm and from 7 pm to 9 pm (10 pm on Friday and Saturday evenings). From New Year to Easter the pub is closed for food on Mondays. If you plan to arrive as a group, telephone beforehand so your meal can be ready for you. Telephone: 01458 860225.

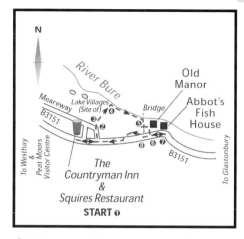

### The Walk

① Turn left from the front door of the pub. Pass the first road on the left. Take the second road on the left, signed 'Meareway'.

② When the Meareway bends left keep straight on through a gate, following the footpath sign. Cross a farmyard, go through another gate and continue over the field ahead. Cross a wooden bridge with stiles at either end and keep straight on with a hedge on your right.

③ Bear a little right to cross the meadow to the bank of the River Bure. Over the meadow to your left are the sites of the Iron Age lake villages. After excavation, the sites were covered and only low mounds are now visible.

④ Turn right to walk along the river bank through a series of gates. On your right long, narrow meadows divided by rhynes slope up to the houses of the village lining the ridge, a pattern that can have changed little with the centuries.

⑤ When you come to a stone bridge turn right through a gate and walk up the concrete approach to a farm. Go through the right hand gate of the two ahead and continue with a hedge on your right through the next gate. Bear left through another gate to pass the farm buildings of

*Medieval hinges on the door of Meare church*

the old manor. Turn right just before the gate leading to the old manor to walk up a narrow grassy path with the churchyard on your right to the main road.

⑥ Turn left, passing the old manor on your left. It was built around 1340 by Abbot Adam de Sodbury and altered and extended in the early 16th century by Abbot Richard Bere. A small stone figure of an abbot stands above the porch.

⑦ As the road curves right you will see the Abbot's Fish House, approached by a flagged path on your left. It is believed the abbey fishermen lived on the first floor, preparing and salting the fish on the ground floor. If you would like to see inside, the key can be obtained at the old manor. Turn right to retrace your steps past the old manor to the church on your right. The magnificent iron hinges which fan out across the door are said to be medieval. Inside there is a fine 15th century stone pulpit. Continue beside the road as far as the war memorial.

⑧ With the memorial on your left, follow the pleasant walkway ahead. When this rejoins the main road bear right to return to the pub and your car.

---

## PLACES OF INTEREST NEARBY

The **Peat Moors Visitor Centre** at Westhay recreates life in the Lake Villages with Iron Age huts, canoes and coracles. There is also a reconstruction of the Sweet Track. Open daily, March to September 9 am to 6 pm, November to February 9 am to 5 pm. Telephone: 01458 860697.

# Kingsdon
## A hilltop village with fine views
## *The Kingsdon Inn*

| MAP: OS EXPLORER 129 YEOVIL AND SHERBORNE (GR 518260) | WALK 21 | DISTANCE: 3 MILES |
|---|---|---|

**DIRECTIONS TO START:** KINGSDON IS IN SOUTH-EAST SOMERSET ABOUT 3 MILES SOUTH OF SOMERTON. THE BEST APPROACH IS VIA THE A372. TURN OFF ALONG THE B3151, SIGNED FOR STREET AND SOMERTON. AFTER ABOUT $1/4$ MILE TURN RIGHT FOR KINGSDON. DRIVE INTO THE VILLAGE BEARING LEFT AT THE Y-JUNCTION AND TURN RIGHT, FOLLOWING THE KINGSDON INN SIGN OPPOSITE THE POST OFFICE. THE ROAD CURVES A LITTLE RIGHT AND THE THATCHED INN IS SET BACK FROM THE ROAD ON YOUR LEFT. **PARKING:** THE PUB CAR PARK OR ON THE ROADSIDE CLOSE BY.

Kingsdon is enchanting. Picturesque farms and houses, many built of golden Ham Hill stone and dating from the early 17th century, line a network of narrow lanes. West of the village rises the 70 foot high tower of All Saints' church. Inside there is much of interest including a 12th century font and an elegant Jacobean pulpit. Medieval bench ends are set into the screen of the north chapel and the Ham stone effigy of a cross-legged knight reclines under one of the windows. We follow a lane which rises north of the village to give views to the Mendips, then take woodland paths to return along a hilltop track with more splendid views.

## The Kingsdon Inn

A village as charming as Kingsdon deserves a special pub and this inn could not be more in keeping. It is a three hundred year old, whitewashed cottage with a mossed thatched roof and tiny casement windows. Inside all is as it should be with low beams, inglenook fireplaces, pine tables and cushioned farmhouse chairs. Everyone receives a friendly welcome. Real ales are Butcombe Bitter, Cotleigh Barn Owl, Otter Bitter and a guest from Otter or another West Country ale. Cider is Burrow Hill and there is a well-chosen wine list.

The menu is locally sourced as far as possible. Popular dishes include smoked haddock and prawn mornay and baked haddock fillet with a herb crust. When we called, other meals included braised oxtail in Guinness and chicken breast with smoked bacon and mushrooms in a white wine sauce. Two dining areas are non-smoking.

The inn is open every day from 12 noon to 3 pm and from 6.30 pm to 11 pm. Food is served from 12 noon to 2 pm and from 6.30 pm to 9.30 pm. Telephone in advance if you plan to arrive as a group as the inn is very popular. Telephone: 01935 840543.

## The Walk

① Turn right from the front door of the inn and walk up the road ahead. Follow the road round to the left past the school on the right. The bell hangs beneath a tiny roof, operated by a wheel.

② At the T-junction opposite the post

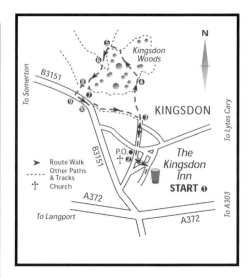

office turn right. Continue past a lane on the right and when the road curves left keep straight on along a grass-bordered lane.

③ Go over a crosstrack and through a gate (a notice asks us to keep dogs on leads) to follow a cobbled track that was once the main road to Somerton!

④ The track curves left as it enters Kingsdon Wood, and then runs through old oak and beech woods, a sea of bluebells in spring. It curves a little right to run downhill and as you near the foot of the hill it turns left with trees on the left. Continue for about 300 yards.

⑤ You come to a footpath fingerpost on the right and a stile with a yellow arrow footpath sign on your left. Turn left over the stile and cross the field ahead with a hedge a few yards away on your left. Go through a gap in the opposite hedge and walk up the next field with the hedge now close on your left.

*Looking towards the Mendips from Kingsdon*

⑥ When you reach the wooded hillside follow the path uphill through the trees. After passing a gate the track becomes wider and leaves the woods at the top of the hill.

⑦ The track narrows and bears right for just a few yards. (It may be overgrown at this point. If so walk parallel with the track with the hedge on your right.)

⑧ After about 50 yards turn left to walk over the grass with a low embankment on your right. This brings you to the B3151.

⑨ Turn left beside the road (there is a verge) for only about 100 yards until you come to an entry into a field on the left.

⑩ Turn into the entry. Do not go through the gate but follow the narrow path on your right running through the trees parallel with the road on your right. The path soon bears left away from the road and becomes a broad hedged track which joins our outbound route at point 3. Turn right to retrace your steps to Kingsdon.

---

### PLACES OF INTEREST NEARBY

**Lytes Cary** (NT) is a small manor a mile west of Kingsdon with a 14th century chapel, a 15th century hall and an Elizabethan garden. Open March to October, Mondays, Wednesdays and Saturdays, 2 pm to 6 pm. Telephone: 01985 847777.

The **Fleet Air Arm Museum** at Yeovilton, south-east of Kingsdon, is an excellent place for a family outing. Open daily (except over Christmas) from 10 am to 5.30 pm (4.30 pm in winter). Telephone: 01935 840565.

# Ham Hill

## An Iron Age hill fort

# *The Prince of Wales Inn*

**MAP:** OS EXPLORER 129 YEOVIL AND SHERBORNE (GR 479169)

**WALK 22**

**DISTANCE:** 2½ MILES

**DIRECTIONS TO START:** HAM HILL IS BEST APPROACHED VIA THE A303. TAKE THE TURNING FOR STOKE SUB HAMDON. DRIVE THROUGH THE VILLAGE TO A T-JUNCTION. TURN LEFT FOR A FEW YARDS (ALONG THE HIGH STREET) THEN TURN RIGHT, FOLLOWING THE SIGN FOR HAM HILL. THE ROAD CLIMBS THE SIDE OF THE HILL. AS YOU NEAR THE TOP LOOK CAREFULLY FOR A JOINING LANE ON THE LEFT. TURN LEFT FOR A FEW YARDS TO A Y-JUNCTION. TAKE THE LEFT HAND LANE, SIGNED FOR THE PRINCE OF WALES INN.
**PARKING:** IN ANY OF THE PARKING AREAS ON THE LEFT OPPOSITE THE PUB CAR PARK.

Ham Hill is the largest Iron Age hill fort in Britain. Rising to a height of over three hundred feet it has been continuously occupied since the Stone Age. It is famous for the beauty of its honey-coloured stone which contributes so much to the charm of many Somerset villages as well as the county's stately homes. Within the ramparts is a fascinating area of little hillocks, the result of hundreds of years of quarrying. Rich in wildlife and plants, Ham Hill is now a country park, and has been designated an ancient monument and a Site of Special Scientific Interest. Choose a clear day for this walk to enjoy the panoramic views from the ramparts.

## The Prince of Wales Inn

This is a large, bustling, very popular inn situated on the top of Ham Hill. There is a comfortable bar with a stone-flagged floor and a cosy 'snug' with plush seating. If you prefer you can eat in the sunny conservatory with superb views. When we called, the blackboard showed a wide choice of food including tagliatelle with fresh tomato sauce, baked aubergines and basil, chicken and apricot terrine with pickled red cabbage and grilled pork and leek sausages with garlic mash and roasted shallots. Lighter meals included baguettes, among the fillings for which were smoked salmon and bacon and Brie. A special effort is made to provide interesting meals for children.

There are local cask ales from Butcombe and Cottage breweries, cider and a choice of wines. Dogs are welcome. The pub is open all day from 11 am to 11 pm on Fridays, Saturdays and Sundays. Tuesday to Thursday it is open from 11 am to 3 pm and from 6 pm to 11 pm. Meals are served from 12 noon to 2 pm (12 pm to 3 pm on Sundays) and from 7 pm to 9 pm. The pub is closed on Mondays. Telephone: 01935 822848.

## The Walk

① With the Prince of Wales car park on your left, retrace your route along the lane towards the road. Just before you reach the road turn right through a wooden gate, following the sign for Stoke Sub Hamdon. Continue ahead, with views into the valley on your left and the embankments

of the hill fort on your right. Scrub is being cleared from parts of the embankments which have become overgrown, to restore the wild flowers. Cowslips in late spring are followed by many rare plants including orchids. The path rises to the north-west spur of the hill fort, which is crowned by a tall obelisk, Stoke Sub Hamdon war memorial. Pause here to enjoy the view. All central Somerset from the Quantocks in the west to the Mendips in the east is spread before you.

② With the memorial on your left, bear right to either follow the path through the former quarry or walk in the same direction along the top of the eastern embankments. This route brings you quickly back through a gate to the parking area where you left your car opposite the Prince of Wales car park.

③ The second part of this walk explores the southern area of Ham Hill. Turn left from the parking area, with the Prince of Wales car park now on your right, to walk round the front of the pub. Follow the lane round to the right as far as the road.

*Stoke Sub Hamdon war memorial crowns the north-west spur of Ham Hill*

④ Turn left and walk along the grass beside the road past Norton car park and Lime Kiln car park.

⑤ Just after passing Lime Kiln car park look for a footpath sign for Stoke Sub Hamdon on your left. Turn left to follow the path downhill past a path on the right. Keep straight ahead, passing a path on your left. The path leads to a small grassy dell with two standing stones. Known as the Timestones, they were carved in 1996 by sculptor Evelyn Body to link the present with Ham Hill's past. The circular stone was inspired by a Celtic bronze bucket mount excavated from the hill. The vertical stone is modelled on a Bronze Age axe head also found on the hill. On midsummer's morning at sunrise, the sunlight shines through the hole in the circular stone to illuminate the axe head.

⑥ Bear round to the left, leaving the stones on your right and following the sign for Montacute.

⑦ Then turn right downhill, still following the sign for Montacute. This leads to a junction of several paths. Turn left with a fence on your right. Go through a wooden gate and turn immediately left to climb steps. At the top go through another gate and turn right to walk past the Prince of Wales pub on your left and return to your car.

## PLACES OF INTEREST NEARBY

**Montacute House** (NT), to the east of Ham Hill, is famous for its long gallery and portraits. Open April to October, Wednesday to Sunday, 11 am to 4 pm. Telephone: 01935 823289.

**Tintinhull Garden** (NT), north-east of Ham Hill, between the A308 and the A303, is open from March to September, Wednesday to Sunday and Bank Holiday Mondays, 12 noon to 6 pm. Telephone: 01935 822545.

# South Cadbury
## In the footsteps of Arthur
### *The Red Lion Inn*

**MAP:** OS EXPLORER 129 YEOVIL AND SHERBORNE (GR 632254)

**WALK 23**

**DISTANCE:** 2 MILES

**DIRECTIONS TO START:** SOUTH CADBURY IS A SMALL VILLAGE ½ MILE SOUTH OF THE A303 BETWEEN WINCANTON AND ILCHESTER. TURN FOR THE VILLAGE OFF THE A303. TURN LEFT AT THE FIRST T-JUNCTION THEN TURN RIGHT AT THE SECOND TO DRIVE THROUGH THE VILLAGE PAST THE RED LION AND CHURCH ON YOUR RIGHT. ABOUT 200 YARDS FURTHER ON LOOK FOR A SIGN ON THE RIGHT INDICATING THE CAR PARK ON THE LEFT. **PARKING:** IN CHURCH LANE CAR PARK.

South Cadbury is a golden stone, dark-thatched village at the foot of one of Somerset's most atmospheric places, Cadbury Castle. It is possible that this Iron Age hill fort was the setting for the tales of Arthur and Camelot immortalised by Malory and Tennyson. History records that after the withdrawal of the Roman Legions in AD 410 a charismatic Celtic chieftain established his headquarters on the hill fort and fought ten battles against the invading Saxons including his last, Camlann, which took place in fields close by. Give your imagination full play as you follow this walk up the lane to the hill fort and enjoy the magnificent views from the ramparts far over the Somerset Levels to the Quantock Hills. Glastonbury Tor, crowned by its tower, rises on the skyline.

## The Red Lion Inn

This is a charming two hundred year old country inn where you are assured of a warm and friendly welcome. The Red Lion is very much a village pub where everyone, locals and visitors alike, is made to feel at home. The comfortable bar area is furnished in traditional fashion with wooden tables and chairs. As you settle happily with your drink or meal you may find it hard to believe any self-respecting ghost could bear to haunt such a pleasurable inn but I was told that a strange mist-like presence once swept through the bar to disappear through a wall!

When we called, the menu included a delicious pork and prune casserole and an enormous mixed grill comprising steak, gammon, chops, kidneys and sausages. Starters included garlic mushrooms and whitebait. Meals are served with seasonal home-grown vegetables. Real ales are Oakhill and a guest ale. Cider and wines are also on offer.

Opening times are from 12 noon to 2.30 pm and from 7 pm to 11 pm. Food is served from 12 noon to 1.45 pm and from 7 pm to 8.30 pm. No food is available on Sunday evenings and the pub is closed all day on Tuesday. Telephone: 01963 440448.

## The Walk

① Leave the car park entrance and turn right along Church Lane towards the village. Just after the first house on the left, turn left up a stony sunken track signed 'Camelot Castle'. As you might expect, the track is known as King Arthur's Lane. Go through a gate and continue uphill through a dip in the lower ramparts of the hill fort. After about 20 yards look up the bank on the left where you will see a cattle trough. A few yards before the trough a small bowl is surmounted by an arch. This is Arthur's Well, where legend tells us his hounds drink deep before following their master along his former hunting path leading to Glastonbury. The track brings you to the central plateau of the hill fort, which covers an impressive eighteen acres guarded by four huge embankments over forty feet high in places.

② Bear right to walk along the top of the embankments, which slope steeply down to the plain commanding the eastern gateway into Somerset. Before their defeat by the Romans, Iron Age people established a flourishing and sophisticated community within these strong fortifications in the first century AD. Excavations in 1967 revealed the fortifications were considerably strengthened around AD 500, the time of Arthur. The foundations of a great feasting hall were discovered and those of a possible cruci-

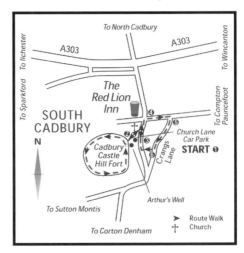

*Castle Lane leads up to the hill fort*

form church, suggesting a Christian leader.

Make your way round the western entrance to return to the track you climbed earlier and retrace your steps downhill to the village.

③ Turn left. On your right you pass Castle Farm House, which dates from 1687, and the 18th century former rectory, now called South Cadbury House. The church dedicated to St Thomas à Becket is on your left. The 14th century tower has a stair turret and fearsome gargoyles. Inside the splay of a window in the south aisle there is an early wall painting of a bishop in cope and mitre, possibly depicting St Thomas.

④ At the crossroads turn right down the lane opposite the Red Lion Inn. Follow the lane a little uphill to Crangs Lane on the right.

⑤ Turn right to follow this attractive narrow way bordered by trees and banks of ferns and flowers in season for about $\frac{1}{4}$ mile, then look carefully for a stile and gate on the right with a footpath sign for Church Road.

⑥ Turn right over the stile. Walk down the field (Cadbury Castle is directly ahead) to rejoin Church Lane. Turn right again to walk the few yards back to the car park.

## PLACES OF INTEREST NEARBY

**Haynes Motor Museum** at Sparkford houses over 300 vintage, veteran and classic cars and motorcycles. It has full wheelchair access and there is a restaurant. Open every day except Christmas and New Year's Day, 9.30 am to 5.30 pm in summer, 10 am to 4 pm in winter. Telephone: 01963 440804.

# Rodney Stoke

## A walk in two worlds

## *The Inn at Rodney Stoke*

**MAP:** OS EXPLORER 4 MENDIP HILLS WEST (GR 484503)

**WALK 24**

**DISTANCE:** 3 MILES

**DIRECTIONS TO START:** RODNEY STOKE IS A SMALL VILLAGE BESIDE THE A371, MIDWAY BETWEEN CHEDDAR AND WOOKEY. THE INN AT RODNEY STOKE FACES THE ROAD. **PARKING:** THE PUB CAR PARK, BUT PLEASE LET THE MANAGEMENT KNOW WHEN YOU LEAVE YOUR CAR WHILE YOU WALK.

Somerset is a county of contrasting scenery. Perhaps the most striking is in the north where the southern slopes of the Mendip Hills rise dramatically above the flat plain of the Levels. The rugged limestone hills and the lush wetland they overlook seem to belong to different worlds. This walk from Rodney Stoke, which lies at the foot of the hills, explores both worlds. We climb the hill behind the village to follow a terraced path with marvellous views and return along a quiet lane through typical Levels scenery, a patchwork of meadows and apple orchards drained by rhynes. Rodney Stoke is an interesting village built of a unique pink stone quarried locally. The church holds memorials to the Rodney family, lords of the manor for over three hundred years.

## The Inn at Rodney Stoke

The bar and dining area of this attractive village inn face west with a wonderful view over the Levels where you can watch the sun go down on summer evenings. In cold weather you can draw a cosy tub armchair in front of a bright fire so here is an inn to enjoy at all times of the year.

Real ales are Butcombe and Bass and home-cooked meals are served every day, lunchtimes and evenings. A wide range of food is on offer from snacks and sandwiches to full meals. When we called, the 'Specials' board featured game pie, salmon fillet in a coriander and lime sauce and Thai green chicken curry. Other popular dishes were chicken and broccoli bake, steak and kidney pie and chicken Madras.

Opening times are from 11 am to 2.30 pm (Sundays 12 noon to 3 pm) and from 6 pm to 11 pm (Sundays 10.30 pm). Meals are served from 12 noon to 2.30 pm and from 6.30 pm to 9.30 pm.

The inn offers caravan and camping facilities, ideal if you wish to explore the Mendips. Groups are welcome but let the management know beforehand. Telephone: 01749 870209.

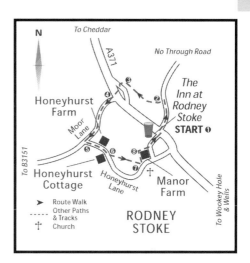

## The Walk

① This walk begins with a rather steep climb but it is well worth while. Cross the road in front of the pub and walk up the road opposite with a no-through-road sign. As you climb there are splendid views west over the Levels and north along the southern slopes of the Mendips. The lane curves left past a gate leading into the Rodney Stoke Nature Reserve with its wealth of rare plants, birds and butterflies. (If you wish to visit the reserve, access is by permit, telephone: 01749 679546.) To continue the walk, pass the gate into the reserve on your right and continue up the lane, which becomes a rough track, for about 50 yards.

② Turn left over a stone stile, following the footpath sign, and walk down the meadow to an iron gate. Cross the stile by the gate and follow the narrow, hedged path ahead. Cross another stile to continue on a more open path which traces the contour of the hillside for almost $1/2$ mile.

③ The path broadens and curves left downhill past houses to a lane. Turn left for a few yards then look carefully on your right for a narrow, hedged path leading down steps. Take this to continue downhill. The path curves left past a path on the right and runs steeply down to the main road, the A371, in Draycott.

*The armoured effigy of Sir Thomas Rodney in the Rodney chapel is dated 1478*

④ Cross the road and follow the narrow path a little to your right downhill to a lane. Keep straight ahead to meet Moor Lane. Turn left to follow Moor Lane to a signpost.

⑤ Turn left along Honeyhurst Lane, following the sign for Rodney Stoke, past Honeyhurst Farm as far as Honeyhurst Cottage.

⑥ Cross the stile on the left opposite Honeyhurst Cottage and bear half-right over the field to a gate in the far right hand corner where there is a stream on your left (if there is a crop you may prefer to walk round the field). Cross the stile by the gate and keep the same heading towards the church tower. Go through a wooden gate and continue towards the tower. Cross a stile to the lane in front of the church. Our way is immediately left

but do visit the church first to see the memorials to the Rodney family.

⑦ After crossing the stile turn left along a footpath with iron rails on the right. Cross the yard of Manor Farm and go through a gate to continue over a stream.

⑧ After about 50 yards turn right through a small iron gate (no sign) and walk up the field ahead with a hedge on your left. Cross a stile to a lane and bear left. The lane brings you back to the A371 beside the Inn at Rodney Stoke.

### PLACES OF INTEREST NEARBY
**Cheddar Gorge and caves** and **Wookey Hole** are within a few miles. For information about the caves at Cheddar telephone 01934 742343 and for information about Wookey Hole telephone 01749 672243.

# Burrington Combe

## The charm of the Mendips

# *The Burrington Combe Inn*

**MAP:** OS EXPLORER 4 MENDIP HILLS WEST (GR 476588)

**WALK 25**

**DISTANCE:** 2$\frac{1}{2}$ MILES

**DIRECTIONS TO START:** THE BEST APPROACH TO BURRINGTON COMBE IS FROM THE NORTH VIA THE A368. TURN SOUTH ALONG THE B3134 AND THE PARKING AREA IS ABOUT $\frac{3}{4}$ MILE FURTHER, JUST PAST THE BURRINGTON COMBE INN, ON YOUR LEFT.

**PARKING:** THE PARKING AREA ADJACENT TO THE INN CAR PARK.

Burrrington Combe is a steep-sided rocky gorge carved by an ancient river which, many thousands of years ago, found a new route underground. It is less spectacular perhaps than the more famous gorge at Cheddar, but no less beautiful with its hanging gardens of ivies, ferns and flowers. From our parking area in the gorge there is a fine view of the massive 70 foot high rock split by a deep cleft in which the Reverend Augustus Toplady sought shelter from a storm in 1762. The experience, it is said, inspired him to write the well-known hymn *Rock of Ages*. Our path leads uphill to cross a broad expanse of bracken-covered moor before we return through woodland past a ruined building with a very strange history!

## The Burrington Combe Inn

This is a really splendid pub for all who enjoy the outdoors. Spacious, bright and friendly it is deservedly popular but somehow the staff always find time to chat and make sure you receive excellent service. The furnishings are modern and very comfortable.

Real ales include Butcombe's and there is a huge choice of meals. You can help yourself to snacks such as Danish pastries and quiche and the full meals on offer when we called included home-cooked ham and eggs, trio of lamb chops, roast leg of pork and chicken with mushrooms, sherry and cream.

The inn is open all day from 10 am to 11 pm and food is served from 11.30 am to 9 pm. Telephone: 01761 462227.

## The Walk

① Return to the road from the parking area and turn left for a few yards to see the Rock of Ages on the opposite hillside. A little further on you will see a cave beyond the rock. This is Aveline's Hole, occupied by hunters around 12,000 BC. Among the objects discovered there were sixty sea-shells perforated for threading into a necklace.

Return to the parking area and walk down the road past the Burrington Combe Inn and the entrance to the Plant Nursery.

② Opposite the gardens cross the road and a track and take the narrow footpath leading uphill to the left of The Cottage. This brings you to a lane.

③ Turn left to continue uphill through beech and oak woods and keep straight on when the lane becomes a track. Through the trees on your right thickly wooded hillsides descend to a wide green valley. Continue past a private track on the right to emerge onto open moorland. Follow the track past a swallet hole on the left known as Rod's Pot, the entrance to one of the many caves and tunnels that honeycomb the Mendips. At a crosstrack bear round to the right and keep on the same path, past two tracks on the left, still bearing a little right. The track runs slightly downhill to a signpost.

④ Just past the signpost the track divides. Turn right to follow a broad way bordered by beech trees. A gate on the left gives access to Dolebury Warren and hill fort, an area of open grassland rich in wild flowers and butterflies. (You could, if you wish, make a detour here to see the Warren then return through the gate to continue our walk.) Shortly the track begins to drop steeply downhill. Look carefully for a gate and stile on the left. Opposite, on your right, you will see a stile leading to a narrow path through the trees.

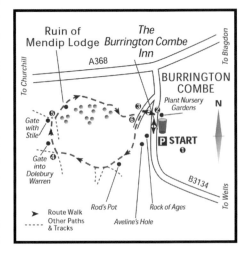

*The ruins of Mendip Lodge, a house with a history!*

⑤ Turn right over the stile and follow the narrow path for a few yards to a broad crosstrack. Turn left downhill and follow the broad track as it curves a little right to bring you to the ruins of a large building on your right. This was once Mendip Lodge, a fine house built in the 19th century by the Reverend Thomas Sedgwick Whalley. Construction on this rocky slope was expensive and the house was decorated with many costly items. Each of the arches along the main front – they still stand – held valuable china jars. Whalley exhausted the fortunes of two wives building the Lodge and after their deaths he married a third time, believing the lady was rich. She proved to be penniless and to add to Whalley's troubles she had charge of her lunatic brother, who came to live at the Lodge and made life unbearable. Whalley could not sell the house and died in France. The Somers family lived in the Lodge until the beginning of the 20th century and after their departure it fell into ruin.

Continue along the track as it leads downhill and narrows before bearing left with a hedge and fields on the left. Go past a wooden barrier to join the lane we followed earlier.

⑥ Turn left to retrace your steps to the path on your right at point 3. Turn right down the hill and right again beside the B3134 to return to the Burrington Combe Inn and your car.

---

**PLACES OF INTEREST NEARBY**
**Blagdon** and **Chew Valley Lakes**, north-east of Burrington Combe, offer many facilities for visitors, including picnic areas and nature trails.

# Wrington

## A walk in the lovely Wrington Vale

# *The Plough Inn*

**MAP:** OS EXPLORER 154 BRISTOL WEST (GR 469629)

**WALK 26**

**DISTANCE:** 3 MILES (TO INCLUDE A DETOUR TO THE WALLED GARDEN)

**DIRECTIONS TO START:** WRINGTON IS A LARGE VILLAGE ABOUT 10 MILES SOUTH-WEST OF BRISTOL. APPROACH FROM THE NORTH VIA THE A370 AT CONGRESBURY OR FROM THE SOUTH VIA THE A38 BY WAY OF LOWER LANGFORD AND BLACKMOOR. THE PLOUGH INN IS IN THE HIGH STREET, SET BACK FROM THE ROAD. **PARKING:** THE PUB CAR PARK.

The northern slopes of the Mendip escarpment give way to a country-side of lush green valleys. Wrington is beautifully sited beside the River Yeo against a backdrop of wooded hills. The centre of the village with its colour-washed Georgian houses and splendid church – the tower so impressed Sir Charles Barry that he used its proportions in his Victoria Tower at the Palace of Westminster – has been designated a conservation area.

Famous former residents include the philosopher John Locke, who was born in a thatched cottage near the church, and the social and religious reformer Hannah More. The walk includes a visit to The Walled Garden, a restored Victorian kitchen garden in the grounds of her former home at Barley Wood, but first we climb the hill behind the village to enjoy a breathtaking view.

## The Plough Inn

This is a most attractive inn. Outside, the walls are colour-washed deep cream and the cottage-style windows are flanked by black shutters. All the family are involved in running the pub and they make sure you enjoy your visit. There is a spacious bar area with comfortable seating and welcoming open fires in winter, and a large separate restaurant. Four real ales are always on offer, including Young's Bitter and Special and Smiles Best. The wine list is comprehensive and there is an interesting range of herbal teas.

Fresh fish always features on the menu, which, when we called, included sole, halibut and John Dory. Other dishes on offer included Old English beef olives and a variety of tempting steaks. In summer the inn is known for its delicious tapas dishes served with crusty bread. You can enjoy these if you wish in the inn's secluded garden.

Opening times on Monday to Saturday are from 10.30 am to 11 pm, Sundays from 12 noon to 10.30 pm. Food is served from 12 noon to 2.30 pm, Sundays from 12 noon to 5.30 pm, and in the evenings from 6 pm to 9 pm. Telephone: 01934 862871.

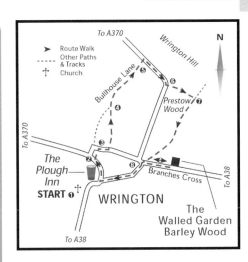

## The Walk

① Turn left from the front door of the pub to follow the road uphill past the pump, which is dated 1885. The road curves left.

② After about 50 yards look carefully for a narrow turning on the right leading to a small iron gate. Turn right through the gate and follow the walled footpath ahead to meet a lane.

③ Turn right along the lane for about 50 yards, then turn left up a narrow lane, passing an intriguing stone-built house with rounded walls decorated with carved heads. The lane climbs past the last houses and becomes a grassy track. Keep straight on up the hill. As you look back there are beautiful views across the vale with the Mendip Hills a purple barrier on the horizon. The track ceases in front of an iron gate. Go through the gate, walk up the field ahead with a hedge on your right and cross a log to join a track, Bullhouse Lane.

④ Turn right to follow the track as it climbs to meet a lane at the top of Wrington Hill.

⑤ Bear right along the hilltop to the point where the lane dips and begins to curve right.

⑥ Leave the lane and turn left through a

*Following the path through Prestow Wood*

wooden gate. Follow a grassy path across the meadow ahead where another gate opens to a wide path.

⑦ Turn right to follow the path downhill through the trees of Prestow Wood to meet a lane at Branches Cross. The tree surrounded by railings commemorates a sad event in Wrington's history. It replaces a former tree on which three ill-fated supporters of Monmouth were hanged by order of Judge Jeffreys after the Battle of Sedgemoor.

If you would like to visit The Walled Garden turn left. Hannah More's house, Barley Wood, begun in 1802, has since been extended but still retains some of its cottage features typical of the period. Here Hannah and her four sisters enjoyed many happy years caring for children and directing Sunday schools. As well as the garden there is a craft centre, a shop and a licensed restaurant.

Retrace your steps to Branches Cross.

⑧ Continue the walk down School Road to join the High Street in the village. Turn right for a few yards to return to the Plough and your car.

## PLACES OF INTEREST NEARBY

**The Walled Garden** at Barley Wood is a fully restored Victorian kitchen garden growing a wide range of vegetables organically. It is open every day from 9.30 am to 4.30 pm and you can sample the produce, as lunches are served throughout the week and at weekends. Telephone: 01934 863713.

**Blagdon** and **Chew Valley Lakes** are a few miles south-east of Wrington (see Walk 25).

# Litton
## A lakeside ramble
# *The King's Arms*

**MAP:** OS EXPLORER 4 MENDIP HILLS WEST (GR 594547)

**WALK 27**

**DISTANCE:** 2 MILES

**DIRECTIONS TO START:** LITTON IS A SMALL VILLAGE BESIDE THE B3114 ABOUT A MILE NORTH OF CHEWTON MENDIP. THE KING'S ARMS CAR PARK IS SIGNED OFF THE ROAD IN FRONT OF THE PUB.
**PARKING:** THE KING'S ARMS CAR PARK.

Litton is an old world village hidden in a fold of the Mendip Hills beside the upper reaches of the River Chew. Today the river is just a tiny stream but once it flowed with sufficient force to power three mills and give the village its name, which means 'settlement by the torrent'. The torrent ceased in 1853 when the Bristol Waterworks Company dammed the Chew above the village, creating two little reservoirs. Now these have become lakes with wooded shores. Lying in this secluded valley, they are a haven for wildlife. This walk follows a terraced path around the lakes, crossing the dam to give a splendid view down the valley, before taking a quiet lane to return to the village.

## The King's Arms

A passer-by on the road could easily miss the King's Arms half-concealed in a hollow surrounded by gardens. But possibly this was a wise precaution as the building has survived for over five hundred years! Inside, the pub is enchanting, its low ceilings crossed by beams darkened with age, and flagstone floors worn and polished by the feet of generations of satisfied customers. A suit of armour graces the main bar, reflecting the firelight in winter, and the mysterious seven faces of the devil can be seen above the bar counter. It is said that Charles II sought refuge in the inn and the ghosts of previous occupants are occasionally seen. One is a lady of noble birth – Charles' friend perhaps? The other ghost is a gentleman.

Meals can be eaten throughout the bar areas or in the separate Garden Room where children are welcome and will find puzzles and colouring books. There is a varied and interesting menu including, when we called, old favourites such as lamb stew and dumplings and intriguing dishes such as peaches and cream chicken and Royal Fish Platter – smoked trout, smoked salmon and prawns.

There are three real ales with Butcombe's always on tap and a good range of wines. Below the inn you will find a pretty streamside garden.

Opening times are from 11.30 am to 2.30 pm (3 pm on Sundays) and from 6 pm to 11 pm. Meals are served from 12 noon to 2.30 pm and from 6 pm to 10 pm (9 pm on Sundays). It is wise for groups to notify the pub beforehand. Telephone: 07968 401364.

## The Walk

① Return to the road in front of the King's Arms car park and turn right. After about 100 yards turn right again down the road signed for Litton. Almost immediately you will see a narrow lane running uphill to the left of the road. Leave the road and bear left up the lane to see the little church of St Mary, built about the same time as the pub. The dark oak pulpit is Jacobean and there are memorials to the Trevelyan family.

Return to the road and continue downhill.

② Just after you cross the stream turn left, following the footpath sign. Cross the stile and keep ahead over the grass. On your left meadows and gardens slope down to the waterside. Cross double stiles and continue, to go over another stile. After about 30 yards look carefully for a stile on your left. Turn left over the stile, walk through a small copse and cross a wooden bridge over the stream. Turn right and go over a stile to Whitehouse Lane.

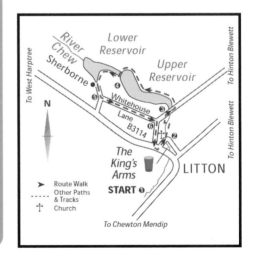

*A peaceful corner of Litton reservoir*

③ Turn right for about 30 yards then turn left through a small wooden gate by a footpath sign. (Ignore a second footpath a few yards further on.) Follow the narrow path ahead with the stream winding through the valley on your left. The water broadens as you approach the reservoir. Follow the tree-shaded path beside the Upper Reservoir to pass a solitary house and small landing stage, then turn left to cross the dam.

④ On the other side, descend the steps on the right and cross the metal bridge over a sluice. Follow the narrow path as it curves right up and down steps to bring you the waterside on the southern bank of the Lower Reservoir, bordered in spring with periwinkles and wild daffodils. The path curves left away from the reservoir to continue to the left of a stream. Cross a stile (ignore footpath signs on the right) and keep ahead over another stile. Follow the narrow path through a wood with the stream still on your right. Leave the wood to emerge on green lawns in front of the tiny hamlet of Sherborne.

⑤ Turn left up a grass and gravel track which shortly becomes asphalt, to a Y-junction. Take the left hand lane – Whitehouse Lane – and follow this to a turning on the right, Back Lane.

⑥ Turn right to follow Back Lane to the main road, the B3114, and turn left for the King's Arms.

### PLACES OF INTEREST NEARBY

At **Chewton Cheese Dairy**, south of the village at Priory Farm, Chewton Mendip, you can view all stages in the production of Cheddar cheese. You will also find a restaurant, a shop and farm animals. Open daily 9 am to 4.30 pm (no cheese-making on Thursdays and Sundays). Telephone: 01761 241666.

# Croscombe
## A dramatic walk through a gorge
# *The Bull Terrier*

**MAP:** OS EXPLORER 4 MENDIP HILLS WEST AND 5 MENDIP HILLS EAST (GR 591445)

**WALK 28**

**DISTANCE:** 3 MILES

**DIRECTIONS TO START:** CROSCOMBE IS ON THE A371, MIDWAY BETWEEN WELLS AND SHEPTON MALLET. THE PUB FACES THE ROAD AT THE FOOT OF CHURCH STREET CLOSE TO THE STEPS OF THE MEDIEVAL CROSS. **PARKING:** ROADSIDE PARKING IN CHURCH STREET. IF THERE IS NO ROOM CONTINUE UP CHURCH STREET, TURN LEFT AT THE TOP INTO FAYREWAY AND PARK ON THE RIGHT.

Croscombe takes its name from Saxon days and means 'the valley of the pass way', a perfect description of the setting of this attractive village. It lies beside the River Sheppey (or Doulting Water as it is known locally), sheltered by steep beautifully wooded hillsides. Many of the houses date from the 16th and 17th centuries when the village prospered as the centre of a flourishing cloth industry. All the weavers needed was to hand: wool from sheep grazing on the Mendips and water to power the fulling mills, which cleaned and finished the cloth. This prosperity is reflected in the church with its splendid Jacobean woodwork. The walk leads northeast from the village through a gorge, its massive rock walls hung with ferns and ivies. Meadow paths and a quiet lane take us back to the village.

## The Bull Terrier

There is a welcome for everyone in this historic village pub. The main building follows the traditional pattern of a medieval house with a central stone-flagged passage, and was built towards the end of the 15th century. The Inglenook bar was once the main hall. The fireplace and ceiling date from the 16th century. There is another bar, a cosy snug and a non-smoking family room. The pub has been licensed since 1612 and as you would expect in so venerable a building there is no shortage of ghosts. Beware the shadowy shapes of monks drifting across the floor of the Inglenook bar!

There is a choice of four traditional ales, including Butcombe, and the pub is well known for its excellent house wines. When we called, an extensive menu included home-made pâté, smoked trout terrine, chilli con carne and filo prawns in garlic dip. Basket meals, sandwiches and ploughman's provide lighter alternatives.

There is a pretty walled garden with attractive views. Opening times are from 12 noon to 2.30 pm and 7 pm to 11 pm (10.30 pm on Sundays). Food is served from 12 noon to 2 pm (1.45 pm on Sundays) and 7 pm to 9 pm (9.30 pm on Fridays and Saturdays). In winter, from 1st October to 31st March, the pub is closed on Mondays and no food is served on Sunday evenings. Overnight accommodation is available. Telephone: 01749 343658.

## The Walk

① Turn right from the front door of the pub opposite the remains of a fulling mill.

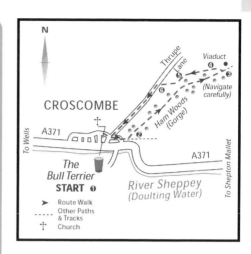

Pass the 14th century market cross and turn right again up Church Street. At the top turn right to walk along Pound Fold, then, bearing a little left, continue along the top of Rock Street and into Boards Lane, which narrows and runs beside a fence on the right. Leave the lane when it turns sharp right and keep straight on to a stone stile. Cross the stile and follow the footpath ahead, signed for Ham Woods. The path follows the open hillside then drops steeply into a wooded glen.

② At the foot of the hillside bear left along a grassy path. Go through a gate and follow the old half-grassed cobbled track leading through Ham Woods, a mysterious gorge home for many wild creatures including deer. Follow the path through the gorge for about 1½ miles to the point where the track becomes a woodland path.

③ Navigate carefully here! Look carefully on your left through the trees for a wooden post marked with a yellow arrow and signed for Wells. (The path is just before you see a tall viaduct on your left.)

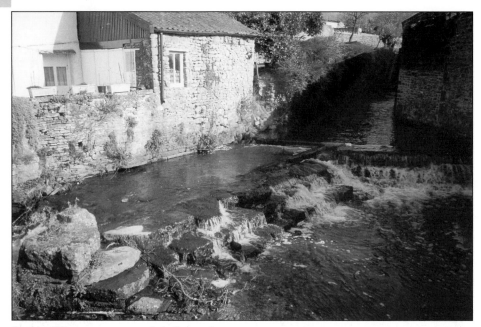

*Doulting Water pours over a weir in Croscombe*

Turn left to follow the path uphill and cross the stile at the top.

④ There is no clear path but follow the direction of the footpath arrow half-left up the field ahead and continue along the hillside, with the woods over the grass on your left and a hedge up the hill on your right. Cross double stiles and keep the same heading to the far right hand corner of the next field. Cross a stile and keep ahead to the corner of the woods on your

---

**PLACES OF INTEREST NEARBY**

The historic cathedral city of **Wells** is close by. For further information telephone the Tourist Information Centre: 01749 672552.

---

left. Continue with the woods on your left and go over a stone stile. Keep ahead over the next field to cross a stile.

⑤ Still no clear path but turn half-right over the field to cross a stone stile (it is about 30 yards to the left of a large gap in the hedge). Continue the same heading diagonally across the next field to cross another stone stile by a solitary tree and reach Thrupe Lane.

⑥ Turn left along the lane, high with beautiful views, before following it downhill to meet Rock Lane. Bear right then left to the main road. To see the river turn left for a few yards, then retrace your steps to return to the pub and your car.

# Mells

## A hidden valley in the Mendips

# *The Talbot Inn*

**MAP:** OS EXPLORER 5 MENDIP HILLS EAST (GR 727493)

**WALK 29**

**DISTANCE:** 3½ MILES

**DIRECTIONS TO START:** MELLS IS ABOUT 3½ MILES WEST OF FROME AND IS NOT EASY TO FIND. THE BEST APPROACH IS VIA THE A361. TAKE THE TURNING FOR NUNNEY. DRIVE INTO THE VILLAGE AND TURN LEFT OVER THE BRIDGE, WITH NUNNEY CASTLE BEYOND THE HOUSES ON YOUR RIGHT. HEAD NORTH FOR ABOUT 3 MILES, FOLLOWING THE SIGNS FOR MELLS. DRIVE INTO THE VILLAGE TO THE TALBOT INN, WHICH IS ON YOUR RIGHT. **PARKING:** ROADSIDE PARKING IN MELLS OPPOSITE THE INN.

Mells, tucked away in the lush countryside of the eastern Mendips, is one of Somerset's most beautiful and historic villages. The 104 foot tower of the church with its triple windows and slender tapering pinnacles soars above the village. Almost all the houses are old, built of golden stone, with mullioned and transomed windows. Leading from the High Street to the church is New Street, bordered by rows of weavers' cottages built by Abbot John Selwood of Glastonbury in the mid 15th century. The establishment of fulling mills beside the Mells River as early as the 13th century had made the export of finished cloth possible and the village prospered, weaving and processing wool from the Mendips and the Wiltshire downs. The walk leaves the village to explore the Wadbury Valley, a thickly wooded gorge beside the Mells River.

## The Talbot Inn

The Talbot Inn can trace its history from 1492. Once coaches carrying passengers between Bath and Wells clattered through its central archway into the cobbled courtyard. Over the centuries the inn has gradually acquired many fascinating features. A high-beamed tithe barn has been restored to house the public bar. To the left of the courtyard the main restaurant has low, oak-beamed ceilings, stripped pews and wheelback chairs and fresh flowers on the tables. The other restaurant at the front of the inn is furnished with tall box settles and solid oak tables.

If you enjoy real ale make your way to the tithe barn, where you can enjoy several brands of Butcombe ales straight from the barrel. Smiles and Fuller's London Pride are also on offer. Delicious meals, for which the inn has a well-earned reputation, are served in the restaurants. The lunchtime menu when we called included hand-carved local ham with free-range eggs, and tagliatelle with smoked salmon in a herb cream and mushroom sauce. Evening dishes included roast best end of English lamb served with ratatouille on a basil sauce and breast and confit leg of Gressingham duck with a blackcurrant and orange sauce. A wide choice of fish dishes is also available.

Opening times are from 12 noon to 2.30 pm (Saturday 3 pm) and from 6.30 pm to 11 pm. Meals are served from 12 noon to 2 pm and from 6.45 pm to 9.15 pm. The Talbot has an attractive secluded cottage garden. Overnight accommodation is also available. Telephone: 01373 812254.

## The Walk

① Leave the front of the inn on your left and turn left along New Street to the church. Enter by the fan-vaulted south porch. Among the church's treasures is a Norman font and you can see some fine work by modern artists. The most striking is an equestrian statue of Edward Horner, heir to the manor of Mells, killed at the Battle of Cambrai in 1917. It is a rare sculpture by Sir Alfred Munnings and stands on a plinth designed by Sir Edwin Lutyens. For a splendid view of the church and the manor house, the home of the Earl of Oxford and Asquith, follow the line of yews north of the church, cross the stile and walk a short distance up the meadow.

Retrace your steps along New Street and turn left. The road runs downhill, curving right past the post office. Pass the lane to Buckland Dinham on the left.

② Turn left along the road signed for Great Elm. After about 300 yards turn right, following a footpath leading through the Wadbury Valley, a dramatic gorge with

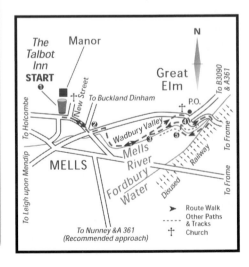

*The lane to the church in Great Elm*

the Mells River running through the trees on the right. After about ¹/₂ mile you come to the ruins of one of the Fussells edge-tool works, a thriving local business with an international reputation until its closure in 1894. The path divides at this point – be sure to take the left hand path, which leads to a post indicating a bridleway on the left and a footpath on the right.

③ Continue up the bridleway, which climbs the hillside to meet the Great Elm road. Bear right beside the road until you come to a small green and a lane to Great Elm church on the left.

④ Leave the road here and turn right opposite the village hall down a narrow lane marked with a weight limit. The lane curves left then right to cross a bridge over the Mells River at the point where it is joined by a stream, Fordbury Water.

Immediately after crossing the bridge turn right through a gate and follow the footpath straight ahead. After about 100 yards, just before the barred approach to a railway, turn right to cross a small bridge over Fordbury Water to a crosspath. Turn right and follow the path as it curves left to run beside the Mells River on your right. After about ¹/₂ mile turn right to cross the river by a wooden railed bridge to a crosspath.

⑤ Bear left beside the river and continue until you meet the outbound route at point 3. Retrace your steps through the gorge, turning right in Mells to return to the Talbot Inn and your car.

### PLACES OF INTEREST NEARBY

**Nunney Castle**, south of Mells, is a massive rectangular moated tower built by Sir John de la Mare in 1373. Open access.

# Wellow

### History comes alive in the Wellow valley

## *The Fox & Badger*

**MAP:** OS EXPLORER 5 MENDIP HILLS EAST (GR 741583)

**WALK 30**

**DISTANCE:** 3 MILES

**DIRECTIONS TO START:** WELLOW LIES ABOUT 4 MILES SOUTH OF BATH. IT IS SIGNED OFF THE A367 BATH TO EXETER ROAD. APPROACHING VIA THE A36 FOLLOW THE SIGN FOR HINTON CHARTERHOUSE AND WELLOW. DRIVE STRAIGHT OVER THE CROSSROADS IN HINTON CHARTERHOUSE AND CONTINUE ALONG WELLOW LANE FOR ABOUT 2 MILES. **PARKING:** IN WELLOW SQUARE, CLOSE TO THE INN.

Wellow is an attractive village built on the crest of a south-facing escarpment overlooking a landscape of gently rolling hills. From the village, lanes run steeply downhill to the Wellow Brook, which is crossed by a narrow packhorse bridge. The village has a long history. The site of a Roman villa has been discovered nearby and it is possible that the present 14th century church, dedicated to St Julian, a Roman saint, stands on the site of a much earlier building. But three thousand years before the coming of the Romans, people of the New Stone Age made their homes among these hills. Beyond the Wellow Brook, their great communal tomb, the Stoney Littleton Long Barrow, lies like a stranded whale on the hillside. This walk leaves the village to visit the barrow and enjoy splendid views over the valley.

## The Fox & Badger Inn

This traditional country pub has a comfortable flagstoned bar with small winged settles tucked into snug alcoves. Blazing log fires greet you on chilly days. But welcoming as the Fox & Badger undoubtedly is, do not be tempted to stay too long! I was told that in the days when a Sheep Fair was held in Wellow Square a married man disappeared into the pub and did not reappear for two days. As he presumably staggered out he was met by his wife, Mary Ann, who was none too pleased. The result gave rise to the rhyme:

> 'Mary Ann killed a man
> With a reaphook in her hand
> Well, well, well, I do declare
> Two days after Wellow fair.'

Perhaps the Fox & Badger's well-kept ales were some compensation. Four real ales are on offer: Butcombe, Badger, Sussex and Bass. In the bar or the separate restaurant you can enjoy some delicious meals, often sourced from local farms. When we called, the menu included rabbit with walnut and brandy sauce, rack of pork ribs, wild duck breast in an orange sauce and the special 'Badger Burger' served with onion sauce and salad.

Opening times on Monday to Thursday are from 11.30 am to 3 pm and from 6 pm to 11 pm. On Fridays, Saturdays and Sundays the pub is open all day. Food is served on Monday to Saturday from 11.30 am to 2 pm and from 6 pm to 9.30 pm, Sundays from 12 noon to 2.30 pm and from 7 pm to 9 pm. Telephone: 01225 832293.

## The Walk

① From the Square walk through the village along the road heading south-west for Radstock.

② After about ¼ mile turn left along a narrow lane signed for Stoney Littleton Long Barrow. Follow the lane as it winds its way downhill into the valley of the Wellow Brook. The furrows and embankments on the hillside ahead reveal the presence of farming communities as far back as the New Stone Age.

③ Opposite a farm in the valley turn left to cross a bridge over the Wellow Brook, following the Long Barrow sign. Turn immediately left again, indicated by another sign for the Long Barrow, and go over a stile to climb the hillside with a hedge on your left.

④ Halfway up the hill look for a stile on your left. Cross the stile and turn right to continue for about 200 yards, with the

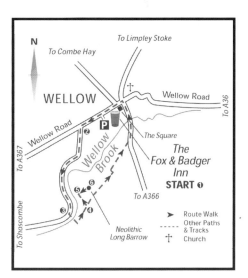

*The packhorse bridge and ford at Wellow*

hedge now on your right, to another stile on your right.

⑤ Turn right over the stile, cross a small field and go over another stile to the Long Barrow. The earth covering of this impressive barrow conceals a huge stone-built tomb over 50 feet in length, skilfully constructed with a central passageway and side chambers in which the dead were laid. The tomb must have served many generations since it was built three

### PLACES OF INTEREST NEARBY

**Norwood Farm** at nearby Norton St Philip, south-east of Wellow, is a mixed farm with many rare breeds. It also has a shop and a café. Open March to September daily, 11 am to 5 pm. No dogs. Telephone: 01373 834356.

thousand years before the birth of Christ.

⑥ From the Long Barrow retrace your steps over the stiles, turning left to return to the hillside at point 4. Turn left and continue up the hill, with the hedge again on your left. At the top of the hill go through a gate on your left and bear a little right to continue the same heading along the top of a field, the hedge now on your right. When the hedge ceases keep straight on and go through a gap in a hedge to join a hedged track. Follow this as it leads gradually downhill to a lane. Continue downhill and follow the lane as it curves left to a ford over the Wellow Brook. Cross the packhorse bridge to the left of the ford and walk up the lane ahead to join the main street in Wellow. Turn left to the Square.